Celebrating Success!™
Fourteen Ways to a Successful Company

Ronald Finklestein

Edited by
Josephine Gilmore of Group Gilmore

With Contributions by
John Bothwell, The Bothwell Group;
Charles Gilmore, Avantt Consulting;
Ivana Taylor, ThirdForce Marketing

Celebrating Success!™
Fourteen Ways to a Successful Company

Ron Finklestein
Learn fourteen ways to help your company become more successful!

All rights reserved.
Copyright 2005

Cover design and book layout by Bonnie Bushman
bbushman@bresnan.net

Morgan James Publishing, LLC
1225 Franklin Ave. Ste 325
Garden City, NY 11530-1693
800-485-4943
www.MorganJamesPublishing.com
info@MorganJamesPublishing.com

This book, or parts thereof, may not be reproduced in any form without permissions from the author.

Habitat for Humanity®
Peninsula
Building Partner

Finklestein, Ron. 1952-
    Celebrating Success!/ Ron Finklestein
    ISBN 0-9768491-5-1 (hardcover)
    ISBN: 1-933596-34-1 (paperback)
Library of Congress Control Number: 2004096506

Dedication

To my son Aaron; may the contents of this book help him eliminate the same mistakes I made in starting my business.

ATTITUDE & BEHAVIORS OF SUCCESSFUL BUSINESS OWNERS

The attitudes and behaviors of successful business owners are well understood. In this special report you will better understand and walk away with specific action steps that you can take and implement immediately. You will learn how to:

- Take action that will change your behavior.
- Change the focus of your business to one of predictable business growth.
- Understand what success people do and how you can implement these actions in your life.
- Identify the behavior styles of people you work with so your relationship with them improves.

To receive this report send a email with the words Free Report in the subject line to info@yourbusinesscoach.net

Having dreams is not the same as living them.

- Ron Finklestein

TABLE OF CONTENTS

Acknowledgement ix
Introduction xi
Attributes of a Successful Company 1
   Creating a Company Culture 7
   Customer Service 13
   Work/Life Balance 19
   Discipline 23
   Attitude 27
   Risk Taking 33
   Business Strategy 37
   Financial and Budget 55
   Business Process Improvement 61
   Information Technology 69
   Marketing 77
   Sales 83
   Training 99
   General Advice 105
   Bringing It All Together 107
Conference Stories 111
   Allergy and Respiratory Center 111
      Health Care *111*
   Aztek 113
      Marketing Communication - Web Site Design *113*
   Bonnie Cohen Ceramic Design 114
      Ceramic Tile & Creative Design for Endowment &
      Fund Raising *114*

Bright.Net **116**
   Innovation and Reaching Out *116*
Brulant **117**
   Profitability *117*
Cardinal Commerce **118**
   Innovation and Reaching Out *118*
Continental Cuisine **119**
   Mediterranean Restaurant *119*
DecisionPoint Marketing and Research **120**
   Market Research and Consulting Services *120*
Interactive Media Group **121**
   Innovation *121*
United Security Management Services, Inc. .. **122**
   Security Guards and Related Support Software *122*
Unicall International Inc. **124**
   Integrated Marketing *124*
TimeWare, Inc. **125**
   Innovation *125*
RADcom, Inc. **126**
   Profitability *126*
Software Answers **127**
   Innovation *127*
Tell Companies, Ltd. **128**
   Innovation *128*
Neighborhood Manufacturing **130**
   Innovation *130*
Professional Travel Inc. (PTI) **131**
   Comprehensive Travel Management *131*

NCS DataCom **132**
  Managed Integrated Network Services Provider *132*
OnlyOne **133**
  Managed Communication Services *133*
5iTech **134**
  Innovation and New Markets *134*
MrExcel.com **136**
  Microsoft Excel Knowledge and Application Development ..*136*
Gateway Title **137**
  Reaching Out *137*
Physicians Medical Service Bureau, Inc. **138**
  Reaching Out *138*
Foundation Software **139**
  Profitability *139*
OEConnection **141**
  Automotive OEM Parts Ordering Process and Software *141*
Fortney & Weygandt, Inc. **142**
  General Contracting (Construction) *142*
ICBS, Inc. **143**
  Web Hosting, Development, and Internet Healthcare *143*
Lazorpoint, Inc. **145**
  Network Engineering Services *145*
Mustard Seed Market & Café **146**
  Full Service Health Food Store *146*

Company Contact Information 149
About the Authors 153
  Ronald Finklestein **153**
  Charles M. Gilmore **154**

Ivana Taylor 156
John Bothwell 157
Josephine Gilmore 158
Conference Stories Author 159
Chris King President/Owner 159
Barbara Payne 160
Index 163

Acknowledgement

This Greater Akron Business Conference and the resulting book would not have been possible if it weren't for the help and dedication of many people. The first person I would like to mention is Don Philabaum, President of IAC. Don had this idea and though it took two years for him to find the right people, he did not let the dream die.

I spent a lot of time trying to find volunteers and it was difficult simply because of the newness of the event. I could not give any assurances about the time commitment. That did not frighten Jo Gilmore, Managing Partner of Group Gilmore. Jo was the project manager for a similar event while in graduate school. Her skill was critical in making this event as successful as it was.

After Jo accepted, it was easier to recruit volunteers. It did not take long for several to volunteer their efforts. Several committee members handled interviews and information-gathering tasks. Thank you Anita Campbell, Thomas McNamara, Holly Corwon, and Chris Vacca. Holly also doubled as our marketing point person. Tom doubled as sales strategist and Anita did double duty in handling the budget.

After all the interviews were finished, Chris King and Barbara Payne took the interview notes, marketing collateral and nomination forms and wrote the stories that were used by the judges. Those stories are at the back of this book.

Leslie Unger made herself available to coach each presenter if they wanted it.

Pete Effinger orchestrated all the hardware and presentation materials. Alice Hall was responsible for the managing the event-day volunteers. Jean Wales did a super job of managing all the day-of-event activities.

Finally, I want to thank all our sponsors. Without their help and support this event would not be possible: Westfield Bank, Westfield Creative, Greater Akron Chamber, Smart Business, IAC, Kent State, TenthFloor, MCPc, American Express, and Air Tran.

Special thanks to Ivana Taylor, John Bothwell and Charles Gilmore for their contribution to this book. In addition, I would like to thank www.2uNews.com for the support I have received in hosting my web site www.yourbusinesscoach.net and the creation of my electronic newsletter.

INTRODUCTION

This book came about as a result of the Greater Akron Business Conference, held in Akron, October 2003.

We got together to do this program because we were tired of hearing bad news. Many of us worked with smaller companies and we knew the negative news we were hearing was not reflective of the successes achieved by these companies.

At the time, a local newspaper was running headlines that looked a lot like: '100,000 Manufacturing Jobs Lost,' as well as stories about Fortune 1000 companies OfficeMax and Roadway being purchased by out-of-state companies. I knew what was being reported by the local media did not reflect the local economy.

In addition, the Information Technology sector throughout the U.S. was in a depression, and thousands of jobs were lost. In Northeast Ohio, many people were looking for jobs, and realizing there were none; many either moved out of the region or started their own companies.

I realized if Northeast Ohio was to continue to be a vibrant place where people wanted to live, something needed to be done over and above what the local government was doing. I wanted to get involved and was determined to give something back to the community where I lived in for so many years.

As part of this effort to give back, a Northeast Ohio Software Association (NEOSA) chapter took form in the Akron/Canton area, called the NEOSA Business & Technology Group. One of the main purposes of this chapter was to create revenue opportunities for the Business & Technology Group members through networking events, educational seminars and workshops.

The original idea for the event that would become the Akron Business Conference came from Don Philabaum, then-President of Canal Technology Group, a group of companies that worked within the community on non-profit activities.

As the NEOSA chapter took form, Don approached me about NEOSA's Business & Technology Group working to sponsor an event that focused on small businesses that successfully used technology to grow. I liked the idea and the rest is history.

The Akron Business Conference was born from a desire to make a difference. The conference would highlight the success of smaller companies in the region and encourage conference attendees to purchase services from local companies. From what I could see, the region had more than enough resources and there was no reason for any local company to spend their money on products and services outside the local region.

Don and I were fortunate enough to have some very senior and experienced business people volunteer. I was very surprised by the number of people who wanted to be involved in this activity.

It took the planning committee some time to determine a theme. A number of good ideas surfaced, but nothing that we were all enthusiastic about. I remember very clearly Tom McNamara saying that the reason we are here was to celebrate the success of these companies. We knew immediately that that was the name we wanted, Celebrating Success!

In working through the conference details, it became clear that the future is not in large Fortune 2000 companies. The future is in the thousands of new companies that are being started every day.

To do this we felt it was time to start a change in regional consciousness by showcasing companies that no one had heard of, but were doing well. These companies were the future of our regional economy. They were doing well and holding their own.

What we did not expect or fully understand was that almost every company had overcome overwhelming odds and moved past some very large obstacles at some point in their existence. I was amazed by their candor concerning the challenges they faced, the opportunities they identified and the transformation that was required to move forward. For many of these companies and their owners, it was both a personal and organizational transformation.

The nomination process was simply. For each nomination received, an interview team talked with the company to ask a set of clarifying questions. After interviewing these companies and reading the interview notes, I started seeing some common threads. I did this to get a first-hand look at what made these companies successful. It was then that I realized that others might be interested in the results. It was actually suggested to me by Ivana Taylor that I should put the results in book form so others could benefit from it.

This understanding revealed several things about leadership. I learned about how important it was to be focused, to believe in yourself and your products. I learned that many of these successful companies did things for their communities and for their customers, because it was the right thing to do. And perhaps most of all, I learned the value of having external advisors and listening to them.

One illustration of "doing the right thing" was demonstrated by ICBS, a local firm providing Internet services. ICBS created a web site, www.holisticonline.com, to help individuals better understand alternative medicines. H e did this because his physician wife's patients were asking about therapies they found over the web that were potentially dangerous. She felt they needed a place where they could get reliable information free from subjective input. This web site is totally supported by him, his wife and group of very dedicated individuals who see the value in the service they are providing. This service is free all who choose to use it.

Another company, Software Answers, www.software-answers.com, made a commitment to their clients. The economy was bad and they were running out of cash. Knowing that meeting expectations would cost more than initially expected, they could have backed out of the deal and left their customers hanging. What they did was to continue forward and honor their commitment because it was the right thing to do. Somehow, they found the cash, met their clients' expectations and held on to their core values. Everything worked out for them, taking the high road paid off.

The founders of the Mustard Seed Market & Café, www.mustardseedmarket.com, an organic health food store and restaurant, have a strong belief in service to God. In serving their fellow man, they believed, it allowed them to better serve God.

This belief, and doing what they love, (providing organic food and qualify vitamins) helped them grow into a robust and successful business.

Each of these companies had a story to tell that went beyond the numbers. My hope in writing this book is to inspire, educate and motivate people who have a business or are looking to start a business. This is not a book about finance, numbers, marketing or entrepreneurship. It is a book of hope, belief, and faith of real companies, real people and real stories.

Hope, because I think our future looks very bright. The number of small companies who are prospering was very exciting and inspirational to me.

Belief, because it takes belief in yourself, your product and service to continue moving forward when things are not going well. The owners of these companies had unshakable belief in what they were doing. They believed they had a valuable product or service to provide.

Faith, because there is so much that can go right, usually from the most unexpected places, to help realize one's dreams. It takes work, but it is so much easier when you know you are not alone: that others have been through the same thing and not only survived, but thrived. Many of these organizations are lessons in faith: in themselves, their products and their employees.

It is not possible to talk about all thirty-two companies in detail, and where I received permission, I included the story that was created as part of the nomination process for your consideration. Each story is unique and has a specific lesson. In most cases, the lessons can be applied to any industry. Enjoy these stories and apply what makes sense to you.

Sincerely, Ronald Finklestein President AKRIS
Greater Akron Business Conference Co-Founder
ron@ yourbusinesscoach.net
330-990-0788

Chapter 1
ATTRIBUTES OF A SUCCESSFUL COMPANY

From the nomination forms and interviews, key attributes were extracted from each business that each felt were fundamental to their success.

These lessons have been distilled down into fourteen ways to achieve success. Note that I specifically chose not to say fourteen attributes of a successful company, because each of these companies did not necessarily exhibit all of these attributes. Some companies utilized many of these attributes, others just a few. These attributes are highly interrelated, and break down loosely into 'softer' skills: company culture, customer service, work/life balance, discipline, attitude, risk taking; and 'harder' skills: business strategy, financial and budget, business processes, information technology, marketing, sales, and training. If it did not fall into a specific section, it was included in a section called General Advice. This section includes advice on what the conference nominee felt were important.

My intention is not to reinvent what has already been discussed in other books, but to bring you snapshots of thirty-two companies who were successful and of how they achieved their success. While all these examples came from smaller companies, with revenues of less than $50M, the lessons are relevant to companies of all sizes.

Celebrating Success!

These fourteen attributes could be compressed further but there were some attributes that needed to be addressed separately, such as risk. Depending on the company, the order and level of influence of each attribute variety widely. We will look at each one of these attributes and go into some detail about each one.

Culture is defined as the "integrated pattern of human knowledge, belief and behavior that depends upon one's capacity for learning and transmitting knowledge to succeeding generations."

Many company representatives talked about how hiring the right person was critical and what they looked for when hiring. I don't think any of them used the word culture specifically, but what they were looking for is people who can fit into their corporate culture or who can help shape the culture they wanted to create.

To simplify, these companies wanted to hire employees that expressed a certain attitude or behavior that would make their business successful, both now and in the future. This was reflected in a company's attitude on work/life balance, risk taking, customer service and training. Because of their importance, we spent time on all of them.

Each company profiled realized the importance of **customer service**, but customer service means different things to different people, so let's define it. A customer is defined as "one that purchases a commodity or service." Service is defined as "the occupation or function of one who serves." Together it means providing service to one who buys your product or service. The concept is simple but the implications and implementations can be more complex.

Many of the nominated companies integrated customer service into a company's culture through training and the design and

2

Attributes of a Successful Company

redesign of relevant business processes. In most cases, the business plan dictated how they provided customer service. Once that service level and approach was defined, modifying the business to support the strategy was a relatively easy matter.

Work/life balance was an important issue to most individuals with whom we spoke. Many did not see a difference between their company and their personal lives. They seamlessly integrated work into their personal lives and their personal lives into their work lives. To achieve a balance, they prioritize what they wanted, and worked their priorities.

Discipline was a decisive element for all companies. Some did not call it discipline, but 'focus', 'staying the course', or 'sticking to their core products and markets'. No matter what you call it, it's still discipline. Discipline can be defined "as control gained by enforcing obedience or order, or to impose order upon." It was hard to have discipline if you did not define a plan or strategy that a company can follow.

The **attitude** of key managers (the president, owner or business leader) was one of the most important attributes defined. Attitude is defined as "the mental position with regard to a fact or state, or a feeling or emotion toward a fact or state." Stated plainly, it is the way they looked at themselves, their company, their employees, their products and customers. Many of the organizations we discussed here strongly reflected the attitude of the company president. The president knew if change were necessary it had to start at the top.

Because attitude was truly contagious, it was broken out separately. The attitude of the leader clearly contributed to the corporate culture; all else flowed from that culture. He or she sets the tone.

Celebrating Success!

Each of these individuals (and their companies) took **risks**. Most were calculated risks with a clear outcome in mind. Many bet their livelihood on their company and most realized they must change as the economic climate changed. Each knew it was a risk not to embrace change. The companies who were doing well all embraced change in one capacity or another. Many tried to create a culture of change. Of the companies that actually made significant changes in their organizations, without exception, wished they had made the change sooner.

The single most critical element identified was a sound **business strategy or plan**. Though they are not the same, for our purposes, I use the word strategy and plan interchangeably. The strategy included product development philosophies and strategies, financial goals with an associated road map, and market-orientation with customer-facing strategies. Our focus was not to review the business plan, though many companies interviewed showed us the metrics they used and talked about how these metrics were solid indicators of where the business was and where it was going. Instead, our focus was to understand the specific opportunity upon which they capitalized and how they did it.

Without exception, it would be very difficult to identify the opportunity and make the most of it without a plan that identified the basic elements of the business and defined the direction.

A common theme was the use of a **financial roadmap and budget** – and of course the discipline to follow it! This roadmap told them where and how to spend their money and provided ways to measure the progress. Finance was the cornerstone of most business plans.

Attributes of a Successful Company

Another frequently mentioned attribute of success was the streamlining of **business processes**. The intention here was to increase productivity and reduce cost. Business processes were the way a business does things. Every company has processes; some were clearly defined, others were implicit. Each of the companies talked about the need to continuously improve their processes, to become more efficient and productive, to respond to market changes faster and provide better customer service.

The next attribute is interesting because it is found in almost every aspect of these companies' operations: the use of **Information Technology**. While technology was important, it became apparent that technology does not have to be complex to be effective.

Marketing is something that each company did that allowed them to develop name recognition for their company, product or service. Some relied on referral selling and built their marketing plan around it. Others spent significant time and energy in building a distribution channel. Still others focused on their markets and attacked it with consistency, commitment and diligence.

In some cases, the business owner and the business itself are indistinguishable. The social life of the owner and marketing of the business were many times one and the same for these entrepreneurs.

These companies approached **Sales** very differently. Some depend on referral selling and that was the extent of their sales process. Others aggressively attacked the market with mail campaigns, cold calls and other forms of direct customer contact. This was usually defined by the marketing plan. Most appreciated the concept that selling was a process that could be measured and improved, like all business processes. They talked about the

Celebrating Success!

importance of having a consistent, measurable and repeatable sales process, and they engaged professional sales trainers to help make that happen within their organizations.

Training can be defined as "to form by instruction, discipline, or drill and to teach to make fit, qualified, or proficient." Because we live in world of continuous change, it is more important than ever to implement a culture of continuous learning. Training was a major issue identified. Later we will discuss how training was used and implemented, and how it supported the business strategy.

So much of what was shared could fit almost anywhere in this book, but for simplicity, it is grouped into a category called **general advice**. This could be a book in itself. It is my hope that someone will read this section and take away something that will make a profound difference in how they manage their business.

Let's move forward and talk in some detail about each of these attributes. At the end of each chapter, some questions are asked to see how well you have incorporated a specific attribute into your business. Your organization may be doing quite well in a specific area and not know it. In other areas, you may want to make changes. These questions will help facilitate the process within your organization.

Chapter 2
CREATING A COMPANY CULTURE

As mentioned earlier, a company culture is defined as the "integrated pattern of human knowledge, belief and behavior that depends upon one's capacity for learning and transmitting knowledge to succeeding generations."

Companies looked to create a culture looked specifically to answer this question: "how do I get my employees to express a certain attitude or behavior that is going to make my business successful, both now and in the future?" Areas where these attitudes and behaviors were expressed were in a company's approach to work/life balance, risk taking, customer service and training. Because of their importance, we will spend time on all of them later in the book.

Many of the conference nominees knew how important a corporate culture was for any successful company. Not all of these companies specifically mentioned the word "culture," but all of them tried to create a specific culture through the programs they implemented and the people they hired.

Each of the quotes below was from a company who saw how hiring the right person could make the difference for them.

Hiring the right person can be defined as having the correct skill set, the right attitude and the ability to fit in to the company's

Celebrating Success!

culture. Many of the comments reflected how important it was to create the ideal culture:

"Never underestimate the value and need for hiring and retaining the best employees."

"Build confidence in your clients, your people, your business partners and yourself."

"Surround yourself with good people and employ a team concept."

"Hire as many smart people as you can afford."

"Good personnel hires led to additional good hires; the right person 'on the bus' make all the difference."

"Provide a clear understanding of the company values and define the culture as soon as possible."

"Look for applicants with a good attitude, natural intelligence and a willingness to learn."

"Both the company and employees can benefit when the culture is built on trust and caring."

"Employees learned how far the company and its management team would go to keep good workers. A testimony to the success of a company is the focus on their people; this can be measured by the average tenure of the employees."

One company, **Gateway Title**, focused on creating a specific culture and on hiring employees who were totally in accord with it.

Gateway Title's primary market was homeowners who sell their own homes, called FSBOs, or 'for sale by owners'. After the business was started, significant strategic problems were uncovered. The owner, Rachel Torchia, had all the business

Creating a Company Culture

knowledge necessary to start the business: she understood the market, knew the applications and had good relationships with the primary players.

Rachel's most significant challenge was that she had underestimated the management skills necessary to run a business. In order to overcome this, she employed a business coach who taught her the value of on-going education and provided sound management advice in the people side of the business. She also made a practice of reading books and listening to tapes on management, and sharing them with her staff.

The first book she picked up was *Gung Ho*, by Ken Blanchard and Sheldon Bowles. Rachel felt the book was so important that she had her staff meet every morning for fifteen minutes to read and discuss it. Response from the staff was so favorable that she now makes attendance and participation in this daily meeting a requirement for all employees.

One of Rachel's favorite tapes to review is called *A Day in the Zoo*, where a management consultant compares different types of people to different animals in a zoo.

As I toured the office, Rachel pointed out the different pictures her staff had put up. Each picture reflected a different animal and contained a caption that reflected the primary behavior pattern of people who reflected a specific animal's behavioral traits. Scenes such as this make it clear that her staff enjoyed the meetings; they contributed and integrated the corporate culture of valuing learning into their way of life.

An important part of Gateway Title's approach was to set expectations for employee participation. If any employee decided not to participate in the morning meetings, they are asked to look

Celebrating Success!

elsewhere for work. Rachel is very clear about the consequences during the interview process, so it does not come as a surprise to anyone if someone left for this reason.

Rachel has created a corporate environment where learning and personal improvement are integral part of her business practice. This led to Gateway Title receiving several awards and being recognized by the State of Ohio as a successful small business enterprise.

Another organization that made a very strong impression was a doctor's office: **Allergy and Respiratory Center**, located in North Canton, Ohio.

The difference at this office was clear as soon as I walked in the door. The waiting room does not look or feel like a typical waiting room. Dr. Given's office feels more like stepping into a living room - his living room. Every aspect of the waiting area is designed for comfort and safety. The feeling of the office is one of security, where you knew that you would be cared for well.

The doctor spent years creating a theme throughout his practice to make his patients comfortable. He believed if his patients were comfortable, they would be more open about the activities in their lives that could contribute to their health problems.

The warm, caring culture shown in the physical environment extended to the personnel as well. Each person I encountered was open and friendly. Each person who worked in his office has the same warm and caring approach. Dr. Given's approach was reflected by each of his employees.

The Allergy and Respiratory Center office was overstaffed compared to other doctors' offices. Each nurse spent, on average,

Creating a Company Culture

thirty minutes with each patient, capturing all the necessary details. This information was entered into a custom application that managed all aspects of the office: billing, instructions, medical records and interview notes.

When Dr. Given entered the examination room, he had all the information he needed because it was already captured by one of his caring staff during the interview process. By reading the notes and asking clarifying questions, he was able to better treat more patients, which was what he liked best.

One activity the doctor did not like at all was paperwork. The custom computer system he designed generated all the paperwork electronically, using data captured during the patient's visit – a big relief for the doctor.

The employees like working there. The average tenure was almost 10 years. Some employees were with him 20 years. Dr. Given does a great job identifying what he wanted his practice to "feel" like and he invested heavily to make that dream a reality. All this was working for the patients as well; Dr. Given has less than a 5% cancellation/no show rate.

Summary

A culture was defined as the "integrated pattern of human knowledge, belief and behavior that depends upon one's capacity for learning and transmitting knowledge to succeeding generations."

Questions for consideration:
1. Is your corporate culture clearly defined?

Celebrating Success!

2. Is employee morale high?
3. Is employee turnover low?
4. Is creating a specific culture part of your business plan?
5. Is employee development part of your company's culture?
6. Have you identified (defined) the attributes of your ideal employee?
7. Do you capture your organizational knowledge for future employees?
8. Do you communicate cultural expectations to your employees?
9. Has the culture evolved or has it been created intentionally?

Chapter 3
CUSTOMER SERVICE

> *"It's true. U.S. firms, on average, will lose half their customer base over the next five years. And 68% of those customers will leave because of a bad service experience."*
>
> – Mosaix, Achieving Business Success Through Customer Relationship Management (CRM)

Much has been written on customer service over the years. From the perspective of a small company, customer service can make or break a company almost overnight.

Mosaix goes on to say that "service leaders (companies which provide superior service to their customers) enjoy the following advantages over their low-service (and often larger) competitors:

- They grow twice as fast
- They experience a 6% annual market share growth versus a 1% share loss (they take customers away from their competition)

> *"Don't be content with doing only your duty. Do more than your duty. It's the horse that finishes a neck ahead that wins the race."*
>
> – Andrew Carnegie 1835-1919,
> American Industrialist and Philanthropist

Celebrating Success!

- They can charge 10% more for their products and still take customers away. Because of this, they enjoy a 12% vs. 1% average return on sales.

The numbers definitely show that the practice of providing superior customer service increased shareholder value and created a competitive advantage that is worth the investment. This is especially important when, in many companies, 20% of a company's customers generate 80% of the profits.

If we think about the benefit of building a relationship with a client in human terms, people like to do business with people they like and trust. Not only will a good relationship bring more business from the client, but satisfied clients will be more likely to tell others about the positive treatment they have experienced. This brings referral business to the organization.

Clients will also tell others about bad experiences. This can drive others away from doing business with you and your company.

Industry statistics show that 68% of customers who walk away from a business relationship do so because of poor customer service. This happens at all levels within an organization. In financial terms, this means that a 5% increase in customer retention could result in a 25% to 85% increase in profitability, especially after the cost of sales is factored in.

Let me give you a personal example. I purchased a cordless phone that had an integrated fax machine. After using the phone for 2 days, I realized that battery was not charging.

When I called customer service, the representative told me they would not replace the battery because it was a consumable and all consumables must be purchased. The replacement battery was more than 30% of the cost of the phone. This was a problem

Customer Service

because I expected to purchase a working phone. I felt the company, not me, should absorb the expense of a new battery.

I told them this and they stated, "It is our policy not to replace consumable free of charge." Several calls to the company, including escalating this in the organization, got me the same answer. Finally, in frustration, I returned the phone and decided it would be best if I did not buy anything else for this company – including a larger-ticket item I planned to buy. Their customer service policy cost the company a total of $2700.

As a small business owner, how would you like to lose $2700 worth of business? And it won't be just one lost sale. If your customer service department consistently handles problem-solving poorly, how many $2700 lost opportunities will you have? And how many people will that customer tell about their negative experience?

Without exception, each company in this book went out of its way to service its customers. These firms understood that it costs almost ten times more to find a new customer then it does to keep an existing customer.

Moreover, they knew that their customers were their window into the world. They were better able to understand how their products were used and to respond faster to existing needs. Successful customer service means that every customer should be comfortable giving you, your company and your product a good reference.

Each company understood the trust their customers place in them. Each did what was necessary to ensure a positive and beneficial experience for their customers. The following comments reflected the overall attitude on customer service:

Celebrating Success!

"Stress the importance of strong customer service; never close a door on a relationship."

"All design and development is done by fulltime employees so the customer has many points of contact with all people within the company. All customer questions are answered by the person who is responsible for the issues."

"And always remember, clients don't care about what we think is important!"

"When you stay close to your customer, it is easier to identify a need in the market and focus your efforts on solving meaningful issues for that customer."

Customer Service can make the difference in the level of success a company experiences.

Summary

Much customer service attitudes are driven by a company's culture. What is your company's attitude toward customer service? Is it a necessary evil or an integral part of customer experience? Is customer service considered an extension of the sales organization and an opportunity to create additional revenue opportunities?

Questions for consideration:

Ask yourself what kind of service you provide to your customer.

1. Does this service give you a competitive advantage?
2. Does your product lend itself to self-service? If so, what is the best way to implement this service?

Customer Service

3. How much does it cost you when you lose a customer? Be honest; include sales time, travel expenses, prospecting time, marketing expense, administrative time, lost revenue, and the host of other costs that are specific to your business. Now compare this to how much it cost to keep the same customer. Don't forget to add in repeat business that would not be available if you lost a customer.

4. Are you capturing each contact with the customer: sales, support, customer services and management? Does the entire company understand that each employee is a member of the customer service department?

Chapter 4
WORK/LIFE BALANCE

"The best way to predict the future is to create it."
— Peter Drucker Writer, Teacher and Consultant

"Balance your personal goals and others' expectations."

It became apparent how focused these business people were and how they protected their time. They had clear goals in mind (business strategy), were aware of their time constraints and very selective about where and how they spent their time. Their decisions about time were motivated by how their actions move them toward their goal.

The successful leaders profiled here understood that every person has 1,440 minutes each day, and how they spent this time directly impacted how much got done and how effective they were.

While I was calling these companies to schedule the follow-up interviews, I was repeatedly asked why I was calling, how much time it would take, and the expected outcome of the meeting.

At first I thought this level of detail was a bit strange, until I realized these individuals were highly focused. They were clear in what they wanted to accomplish. If a given activity did not help them reach a specific goal, it is either delegated or politely declined.

Celebrating Success!

Needing to work within the time constraints of these business leaders, forced me to better clarify my message, focus, and get to the point faster. Details were often delegated, allowing these busy executives to make decisions in shorter time frames.

Amy Merrill of DecisionPoint Marketing made this comment during our interview: "Treat time as a precious commodity, because it is easy to get involved and let the business suffer." This comment clearly reflected the attitude of conference nominees and presenters.

This is not to say that these executives do not give of their time. They do. Many are involved in outside charitable activities and these activities were very important to them.

Another aspect that I found interesting was how they managed their time. Repeatedly I would have my call returned after 5:00 PM in the evening, sometimes as late as 9:00 PM. It became clear to me that anything not directly related to the day-to-day operations of the business, or was not a marketing or revenue-related opportunity, was one of the last items to get done in the day.

This implied that there was no such thing as an eight-hour work day. I met with some people early in the morning and others late in the evening. Most did a good job of protecting their day.

Bob Dianetti of RADcom made a comment to me that showed a different perspective on work/life balance. Bob loved what he did and his company was very good at what they do. Bob was able to maintain a different perspective than most. His company was an investment of his time, energy and money. He had very clear expectations of his company to provide the type of lifestyle he wanted for himself and his family.

Work/Life Balance

When his company was not performing to his expectations (still profitable but not meeting planned ROI), Bob asked some of the hard questions about his business. He explained to me that as much as he loves what he does, he treated his company as an investment. This investment, if it did not meet certain personal and business objectives, should be treated as any other investment. It was amazing how he was be so passionate about his business and yet so completely objective.

At first I was surprised by his comments, but as I thought about his statement over the course of several weeks, I realized that this is probably one of the healthiest attitudes I encountered. His priorities were clear, he was focused on the outcome he expected, he took action that was consistent with both his personal and business values and objectives and he knew what he wanted.

Many owners and managers were clear about their priorities and focused on the outcomes they wanted. In most cases, they were clear from a business perspective about the performance they expected, but did not seem to have the personal clarity that Bob had about treating his business as an investment.

Many of these individuals did not differentiate their personal life from their business life. Many of the activities they embraced allowed them to marry both their business and personal lives. Many socialized with their clients and claimed them as friends.

Summary

Owners and mangers of these companies treat their time as their only significant asset they 'owned'. Decisions on how they used this asset were made based on how the activity supported

Celebrating Success!

both business and personal goals. This required clarity of direction and focused decision-making.

Questions for your consideration:

1. Are you clear about how you are spending your time?
2. Are you spending your time on activities that move in the direction of your goals?
3. What changes can you make that would allow you to spend more time on what's important to you?

Chapter 5
DISCIPLINE

This book is about how companies that participated in the conference use discipline as an integral part of their business plan. They use discipline in defining their strategy, implementing strategy, managing to a budget, adapting attitude and culture, and carrying out marketing strategy.

Consider how these comments reflect this level of discipline:

"Stick to what you do best and what you are passionate about."

"Focus on just one or two things – that gets everyone focused. Then don't waste time, just take action."

"Test, fail quickly, and move on."

Each of the conference nominees were very focused in their business. They had their plan and applied the discipline to focus on and work the plan.

Many of the companies had opportunities to engage in activities that were not consistent with their core business. Without exception they passed on these opportunities, all for the same reason: "it is not our core business and it would distract us from what we are supposed to do."

This ability to choose not to follow an opportunity implied that these leaders maintained the discipline to know their core markets and stay focused on those markets. They went through the business

Celebrating Success!

strategy and planning process, and developed a budget to support the business plan. Then they worked the plan.

If they did not approach their business with discipline, they would lose focus and become distracted from the primary objectives.

If they did not follow the activities that needed to be done (based on their business plan), it was difficult to plan their day, week, and month. How do you know which activities that will help you accomplish your goal with out a destination in mind? How do you know if you are making progress? How many resources did you waste chasing after business that may not be a good fit for your company?

Setting aside a regular time for planning was critical. Depending on the individual, they decided which hours of the day were allocated to working in the business and when to work *on* the business.

Of course, they had a huge advantage in running their own business rather than working for someone else. On company's management team did a plan review every Monday at 6:30 AM.

Each of the business owners walked a fine line between working on the business and working in the business. When they were working in the business they were selling, shipping products, or dealing with the endless number of problems that face a business owner every day.

When they worked on the business they looked at the markets, customers, and the financial plan, tracking and modifying it as required. They checked their progress against the plan and checked to see if the plan was still valid. This allowed them to keep the

Discipline

pulse of their clients, competitors, and markets while identifying potential new opportunities.

It was extraordinarily difficult to spend time working on the business when the demands of working in the business were so great. It takes discipline to realize and implement a certain time to create and modify your company's direction.

The major lesson learned was that these business owners did what needed to be done, not what they wanted to do. They dedicated time to focusing on strategic business issues and delegated less significant tasks to others, or moved them to less critical time frames.

These executives and entrepreneurs were very good at determining what was necessary to move forward. They were not afraid to make the hard decisions. It's all very well to set a work schedule and stick to it; it's quite another to spend that time doing what has to be done rather than what you'd rather be doing.

For example, if you spend the first three hours of your peak concentration time reading and responding to email rather working on those hard challenges that required dedicated thinking time, you're doing the right things at the wrong time. Yes, you do need to read and respond to your email, but in most cases email is not an intellectually demanding task. Do it when your brain is winding down, not when it's at its sharpest. Do the hard work when your brain is at its best.

Also, consider letting the answering machine or voice mail answer your phone during planning time. It is easy to get so focused to responding to these interruptions that we let them set our priorities for us.

Celebrating Success!

Don't forget to be flexible in responding to unanticipated changes in your schedule. If something comes up that needs your attention, by all means attend to it. Just make up the time later on. Being disciplined does not mean being rigid.

They knew when to be disciplined and inflexible and when to go with the flow.

Don't forget to reward yourself for getting the job done. Nothing motivates me more to finish a project than the knowledge that when I do, I have full permission to spend time on the other activities that are more consistent with my nature and more to my liking.

Summary

Discipline was about staying focused on your business, on your business plan, and where you want to take your business. It was spending time and resources according to your plan; it was changing your plan when it is not working.

Discipline required knowing when to work on your business and when to work in it. Discipline was also rewarding yourself after you accomplished a particularly difficult task.

Questions for consideration:

1. Are you disciplined enough to define your markets, develop a sales and marketing strategy and measure the success of the programs (to create a business plan)?
2. Do you benchmark your organization against your competitors to measure the effectiveness of your strategy?
3. Do you have a schedule that allows you to maximize your time and effort?

Chapter 6
ATTITUDE

> *"The first key to success is deciding exactly what it is you want in life."*
>
> – W.L. Hunt

Attitude was a choice. We created the attitude we needed that allowed us to move towards our goals. As Napoleon Hill, author of *Think and Grow Rich*, stated:

"Attitude is something you can control outright and you must use self discipline until you create a positive mental attitude - your mental attitude attracts to you everything that makes you what you are."

Charles Swindell makes an even stronger statement and one I am fully with which I fully agree:

"The longer I live, the more I realize the impact of attitude on life. Attitude, to me, is more important than the past, than education, than money, than circumstances, than failures, than success, than what other people think, or say, or do.

It is more important than appearance, giftedness, or skill. It will make or break an organization, a school, a home.

The remarkable thing is we have a choice every day regarding the attitude we will embrace for that day.

Celebrating Success!

We cannot change our past. We cannot change the fact that people will act in a certain way. We cannot change the inevitable.

The only thing we can do is play the string we have. And that is our attitude. I am convinced that life is 10 percent what happens to me and 90 percent how I react to it. And so it is with you."

> *"Choosing to live your life by your own choice is the greatest freedom you will ever have."*
>
> – Shad Helmstetter

What do conference participants have to say about attitude? Their attitudes were upbeat, focused, and determined. All the presenters and conference attendees with whom I spoke shared a desire to learn, and many of them believe in sharing what they learned.

Many companies faced some pretty serious criticism as they created and developed their business. As problems surfaced, any of these individuals could have folded and went to work for someone else.

As one nominee said "don't let criticism get you down [and] don't listen to the people who say it can't be done."

It was important to have a clear vision and "don't let others talk you out of it." All suggested that you follow your dream and "have passion for what you do" and "believe in what you're doing. That makes it fun." Having a good idea was important as well. "Be the best at what you are doing and don't copy someone's idea."

Many of the companies mentioned "Teamwork – the employee bond – as the reason they made it." The team extended to outside help as well: "make the leap of faith and trust your advisors."

Attitude

They also mentioned that "as an employer you have the responsibility for each employee's well being."

> *"Whatever you focus on is what you get."*
> – Anthony Robbins

Others stressed the importance of taking emotions out of the decision-making process, while emphasizing the importance of "objectivity and independence."

Getting a business off the ground required persistence and determination. This was mentioned several times by conference participants.

Attitude was also an important element in customer service. Almost every individual had something to say about customers and customer service: "Customers always have options. So we made sure all of ours were allowed to choose whether to participate in the new functionality or keep it the old way. It was critical to put customer desires first, even if it meant letting them walk away" and "it's okay to charge higher rates and turn down some business."

Almost all of them stressed the importance of goal setting. It was very hard to know where you are going if you do not have goals. Several recommendations for setting goals follow.

1. If you set a goal and it did not work you need to take a look at why this happened. The importance of goal setting was stressed repeatedly. If setting a goal did not work for you, do not stop setting goals; figure out what you did wrong and try again.

Celebrating Success!

2. Goals need to be consistent with our personal values and beliefs. If you create goals that are not consistent with who you are, you will lose interest because you created an inherent conflict between what you want to accomplish and who you are.

3. When you create a goal, it needs to be your goal, not you wife's or husband's, not your mother's or father's. Yours! It needs to be what you want to accomplish! This is most important for your personal goals. Business goals are usually created for you by clients, markets, customers and supervisors.

4. If you can't get excited about your goals you will lose interest in them. They will go by the wayside like a fallen leaf or a rain drop, with no more impact in your life. Create goals that you are passionate about – goals that have some inherent risks.

5. Goals must have some inherent risk involved. If there is no risk involved there can no be sense of accomplishment. If you are not stretching yourself and moving outside your comfort zone, your goals are probably not challenging enough.

6. Many people confuse setting objectives with goals. They can have some overlap but typically goals can be broken down into specific measurable objectives. We may have many goals, but we must decide which one's are the most important and create a plan to satisfy these objectives. Your objectives are the action steps that allow you to move forward – they are not the goal.

7. Sometimes we are so excited about what we want to accomplish we set too many goals. It is just not possible focus on more than one or two. Ideally, focus on one until

Attitude

you have realized that goal. Do not dilute the effort by over extending yourself.

8. Focus on what it looks like to accomplish this goal. Know what it feels like when you achieved this goal. Plant the end results in your mind and body by seeing and feeling the end results.

9. We need to choose what we will think about. Our thoughts support, or should support, our goals. We cannot have a specific goal in mind while thinking about how it won't work.

10. When you control your thoughts you are starting the process of controlling your attitude. Decide what attitude you want and focus on those thoughts.

> *"Thoughts lead on to purposes; purposes go forth in action; actions form habits; habits decide character; and character fixes our destiny."*
> – Tryon Edwards

11. Create plan that will get you where you want to go. Don't over analyze if you cannot see the road ahead. Just get started and you will see the proper course of action to take as you move forward. You can update your plan accordingly as things become clearer.

12. Be persistent! Keep a clear picture of your goal in mind and keep moving forward.

13. Measure your progress. Change your plan if necessary. A rocket going to the moon is always making adjustments to stay on course. It is always measuring and correcting its flight pattern. Adjust your course but keep going.

Celebrating Success!

Summary

What was impressive was the conference participants' positive attitudes and their belief in themselves and employees.

It was a real thrill to be able to discuss the importance of attitude with these capable individuals. Their beliefs and how they used attitude as a business tool to help them through tough times was both inspirational and motivational.

We must always remember that attitude is a choice. You can determine how you chose to react to a given situation. The conference participants were able to see something positive – even while in the middle of some very difficult situations.

Questions for consideration:

1. Do you let your situation dictate your attitude? If you do, take a lesson from the above companies and use your attitude to dictate how you choose to see your situation.
2. The attitude of the company owner or president helps create the company's culture. How is your attitude reflected within your company?
3. Does your company set a goal that helps to create the attitude, while supporting the kind of behavior you want from your employees?
4. If you were in charge what kinds of goals would you set?

I have written a book dedicated to the importance of having a good attitude. It is called Celebrating Success! The Power of Attitude! How to Create More Good in Your Life. If you are interested in acquiring a copy, send me an email (ron@akris.net) and we will make it happen.

Chapter 7
RISK TAKING

"Act boldly and unseen forces will come to your aid."

– Brian Tracy

"Some would suggest that entrepreneurs don't take risks.

"They are so convinced that they have discovered a niche in the marketplace that the idea of failure doesn't occur to them. They are, of course, aware of problems along the way, but they will always endeavor to minimize them." Keith (from the Internet).

An entrepreneur is someone who is a reasonable risk taker, has the self-confidence to take action, is not afraid of hard work, and has goals to measure progress, while holding themselves accountable. I should state here that this statement is not a scientific fact. It is an observation I made while writing this book, through observing the companies and talking to the decision-makers.

A reasonable risk taker is one who defines the opportunity, understands how it solves a problem, and creates and works a plan to address the need. Many of the companies profiled here did their due diligence on the problem or opportunity, understood the risks and had the confidence to move forward.

Self-confidence is an internal knowing. It is a trait that allowed these individuals to move forward when they came to a decision point. It usually comes from having established a track record of

Celebrating Success!

success, or from an ability to take one's past experience and use that knowledge in new and innovative ways.

The business and financial plan is where the goals are defined and measured. Each of the risk takers had goals, measured the goals and took corrective action to keep moving forward (see section on Finance & Budget).

Risk implies a lack of certainty in a given situation. There are three primary risks that a company must deal with: technical, financial, and social.

1. Technical risk is the degree to which it is difficult for an organization to determine the reliability, capacity, and precision of a new technology, or whether newer technology will soon make an innovation obsolete.
2. Financial risk is the degree to which an investment decision (e.g. in personnel, technology or development) will yield an attractive return on investment and whether future returns can be forecasted accurately.
3. Social risk is the degree to which conflict is likely to occur during implementation of an innovation. For instance, will a labor union oppose an innovation because of the laborsaving consequence?

Studies have shown that the most successful people make decisions rapidly. They can do this because they are clear on their values and what they really want for their businesses (and their lives.) The same studies also show that they are slow to change their decisions, if at all.

On the other hand, people who fail usually make the decision slowly and change their minds quickly, always bouncing back and forth.

Risk Taking

Quick decisions can be made and risk reduced when you know exactly what you want your business to look like when it is "done." That is why it is imperative that you clearly define your business' mission and vision and create forward-looking plan. When you plan effectively, decisions become quick – and risk is reduced because the answer to ANY challenge, when analyzed in respect to your goals, mission and vision becomes crystal clear. A decision can be made rapidly, and the actions that flow from the decision can be taken.

Many of the nominees talked about how difficult it was to make some of the decisions they faced. Yet, without hesitation, when asked what they would do different, each one said they would have made the decision and implemented the change sooner.

Studies have shown that people who take financial risks in the workplace generally tend to be more successful in their jobs; a finding which runs contrary to the idea that risk taking is simply self-defeating.

> "Test fast, fail fast, adjust fast."
> – Tom Peters

This does not presuppose that the necessary precautions were not taken. It is important to do a risk analysis, understand each risk associated with the decision and assess the financial impact of each risk. This allows you to create a forward-looking contingency plan. Then, if things do not work out as expected, the obstacle already has a planned response and an alternative course of action.

Celebrating Success!

Summary

Facing risk is an inevitable part of life, of making changes, both in our personal and business life. Know what your strategy is, then accept risks which reward you with progress toward your goals. Good planning and systems can moderate risk.

Questions for consideration:

1. What are the consequences of taking a specific risk (costs, market failure, etc.)?
2. What is the risk of not taking a specific risk (opportunity lost, loss of market position)?
3. Could this change put you further toward your goals?
4. What will you do if your risk-taking fails? Do you have a contingency plan in place? Have you completed a risk analysis?

Chapter 8
BUSINESS STRATEGY

In this chapter we take a look at an often spoken-of, often misunderstood, and not very often effectively utilized subject – business strategy. To condense a subject that is often in the sole subject of a heavy volume into one chapter, I am limiting our discussion to a number of key points:

- What business strategy is – and what it isn't
- How (well) different businesses approach the execution of a business strategy
- A process for establishing your business strategy
- Making business strategy part of your everyday business activities

The objective of this chapter is to provide an overview of business strategy. As noted above, there is much more detail that can be read on the subject; however, like many business activities, the 80/20 rule applies. That is, 80% of the benefit of having a business strategy can be had from a fairly small (20%) effort. The real question one must ask is, "Do I need a really well thought out business strategy in order to differentiate my business from that of my competitors?" In today's business environment that may well be the case – and if so, something closer to a 100% effort may well be justified to ensure that your business is a more desirable supplier to your customers than that of your competitors.

Celebrating Success!

Here are some quotes from conference participants.

"Build a strong foundation."

"Change directions when you hit the wall!"

"Startup managers need a working knowledge of financial metrics and reporting, and especially cash flow management. Develop 'business protection' documents early."

"Build on a solid foundation. Take whatever time is needed to do it right. Plan conservatively. Multiple financial supporters are an advantage over a single capital source. 'Partner' decisions are healthier."

"It is important to have a higher vision and purpose."

"Be the best at one thing."

"Don't try to do it alone – get the best advisors. Then listen to them."

It gave him "comfort that he had the expertise to hire the right preferred vendors, plan for contingencies and execute."

"Don't dream or plan within budget constraints. Most great ideas can be implemented within budget **AFTER** it's been conceived without boundaries."

What Business Strategy Is – and What It Isn't

The term business strategy is one that is widely used, has many meanings to many people and, in general, is not well understood. A good start to thinking about business strategy is to debunk a few common myths:

- *Most business do not have a business strategy*: Contrary to popular belief, *all* companies have a business strategy. For companies who have not thought through their mission and how that will be translated into outcomes with value, their strategy boils down to reacting to opportunities and responding to crises as they occur. Such organizations rarely achieve their full potential and often do not survive.

- *A business strategy is something developed and refined every few years*: No. Highly successful companies are continuously refining their business strategy to ensure their efforts are focused on the best possible targets. Their business strategy is a living, breathing part of ongoing business activities.

- *Only large companies can afford well-developed, well-documented business strategies*: Highly successful companies of all sizes have documented their business strategies in such a way that the entire business organization knows the key elements of the strategy, so each employee knows where they fit into the strategy and how the strategy is evolving with the evolving business environment.

- *Formalizing a business strategy can only be done with the assistance of an expensive externally supported effort*: Certainly outside support can be used to focus and organize the effort to develop a well thought-out and documented strategy; however, many organizations also have undertaken the effort on their own and have achieved significant success.

- *A properly structured business strategy adheres to and is documented in accordance with the Harvard Business School outline of...*: Nope. There are as many formats for successful business strategy development and documentation as there are companies who take the time to formalize the effort.

Okay, so we've agreed that a few of the common myths about business strategies are just that – myths; so what constitutes a

Celebrating Success!

business strategy and how does a company go about refining its strategy to ensure maximum company performance?

A business strategy is the company's fundamental concepts of why it is in business. It defines the what, how, where, who of the company's efforts focus in return for customers' business. Clearly, the more detail, focus and general articulation of this strategy that can be contained in a structured document, the better.

The effectiveness of a business strategy comes down to how:

- Crisp the business definition is
- Clearly the key activities needed to execute that business are defined
- Well the definitions and requisite activities are communicated to those who will execute them

The form a business strategy takes depends on the organization – that is, the format for a one-person organization (and one that is going to stay as a one person organization) can be very different from that of a multi-employee organization. For the very small organization it may be just a few notes on paper or a well-understood approach to business on the part of a few key players. For a larger organization, an effective business strategy is probably documented in moderate detail as the management team develops it with broad employee and outside input, crisply communicated to all employees and regularly (and formally) updated to ensure it evolves as the business evolves.

In all cases, the more thoroughly thought out and the more clearly articulated the business strategy, the more successful the execution.

Business Strategy

A Note on Documentation

While informal documentation is sufficient for many smaller organizations, the process of creating a written record of the company strategic can offer several key benefits:

- It can be a process to clarify thinking, build consensus among key players in the organization and codify agreed-upon results.

- It can validate strategic concepts and the ability to communicate them internally and externally – if you can't write it down clearly, how can you communicate it?

- Once written down, it becomes a useful tool to communicate the strategy clearly and concisely to internal and external stakeholders – employees, suppliers, customers, investors, etc.

- Much like a calendar, a written plan is also a visual reminder of key milestones and tasks.

Writing your strategy down does not, however, mean writing it in stone – this should remain a living, evolving document.

How (Well) Different Businesses Approach the Execution of a Business Strategy

Ultimately, the proof of the pudding is how well the business strategy is executed.

How a business strategy is utilized, like many other activities, is typically found on a continuum – a continuum that runs from the truly excellent at one end of the spectrum to the very poor at the other. As you might expect, the typical company is in the middle of the spectrum and the distribution of companies along the spectrum follows the familiar Gaussian distribution or Bell Curve.

Celebrating Success!

Figure 1 shows the different characteristics of business strategies along a spectrum and characteristics of those business strategies for the different points along the spectrum.

Of course, what level of business strategy excellence is required differs from industry to industry and situation to situation. If your competition does not focus on effective use of a business strategy,

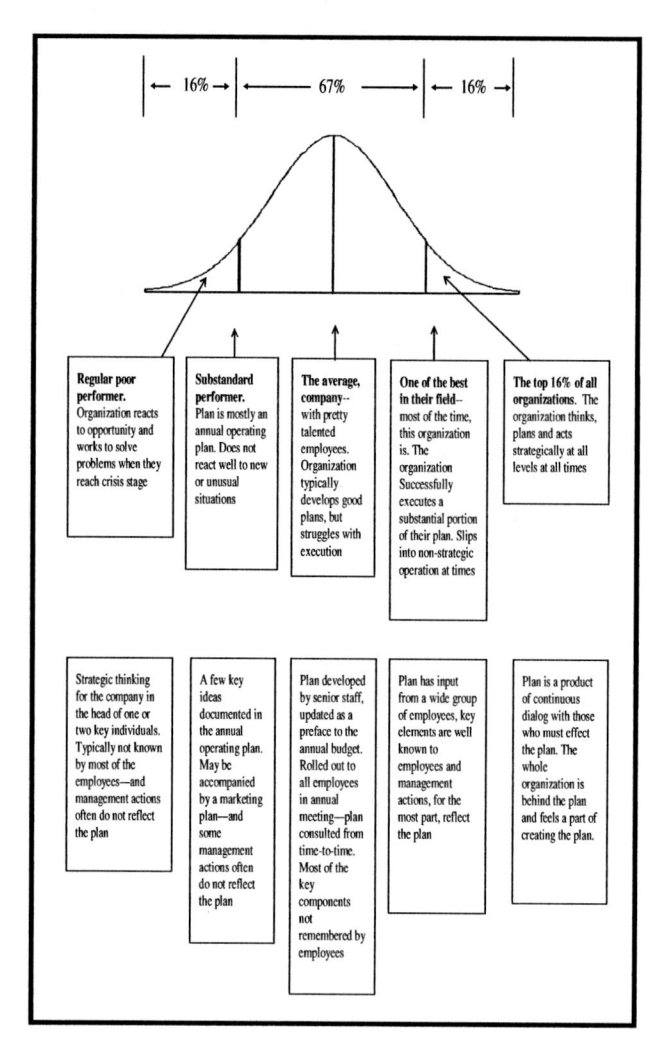

Figure 1

Business Strategy

then you may not be required to do so either. On the other hand, having an effective business strategy when your competition does not, can be a major competitive advantage.

The boxes under the Bell Curve are shown in two rows. The first row describes the business strategy **performance** for organizations in the different areas of the Bell Curve. The second row of boxes describes the **approach** organizations in those sections of the Bell Curve take to the development of a business strategy. As you look at these different characteristics you can easily think of different business organizations you are familiar with and where you might place them on the curve. Clearly, you should also be thinking about where your organization fits on that curve as well. As noted before, this curve is relative. That is, there are few absolutes about the curve but rather the curve depicts relative performance that can be expected within and industry/market.

A Process for Establishing your Business Strategy

So, you have noted your position on the Bell Curve and, presuming you are not in the right-hand one-sigma + area, you have decided you would like to improve your relative business strategy position on the curve. How do you go about it?

There are many different processes that can be used to develop a business strategy – most all of them have the same basic elements. The most important aspects of developing a business strategy are to follow some kind of a process and to understand what it is that you expect to achieve from the different steps within the process. Most importantly, it is imperative that the process of developing a business strategy be something that is in the hearts and minds of the management team – and indeed the entire organization

Celebrating Success!

– undertaking effort. Walking through the steps without a commitment to the end results is a complete waste of time.

A well developed business strategy has:
- Powerful tactics,
- A pragmatic path, and
- Alignment of the management team

Successful companies invest significant time in developing a business strategy in order to make their future vision a reality.

However, it is not uncommon for the process that develops a business strategy to unconsciously limit input, minimize visibility of ideas and fail to resolve differences within the management team. These situations prevent development of the best tactics and priorities for the business and create risk that the management team will not be aligned around actions, roles, and responsibilities. **The plan may sit on a shelf** – and that is a waste of everybody's time and effort and can be a significant contributor to a reduction in morale.

Achieving an actionable business strategy and an aligned team requires **participation** that is broad but efficient; **consensus** created by building on the best elements from many perspectives, experiences and capabilities, and **agreement** achieved through debate, dialog and resolution of differences. Incorporating these elements provides tactics and targets representing the best thinking of the business, and agreement around the goals, path, actions, and responsibilities.

For the best business strategy development, each participant provides their independent thinking to each element of the plan. Group discussion, with the benefit of visibility of the multiple

Business Strategy

individual inputs, usually creates additional alternatives that possess the strength of the entire planning group. Figure 2 illustrates a basic strategic planning framework that can be harmonized with existing frameworks or templates that are in use in your business.

The outputs of such a business strategy development process include:

- A plan summary with key concepts and milestones clearly laid out

THE AVANTT STRATEGIC PLANNING FRAMEWORK

```
                    PRE-PLAN ASSESSMENT SURVEY
                              |
                    BUSINESS FOUNDATION
                    • Business Philosophy
                    • Values & Principles
                    • Vision
                    • Communication Plan

EXTERNAL ASSESSMENT                    EXTERNAL APPRAISAL
• Market Segments &                    • Focus Groups &
  Opportunities                          Employee Survey
• Competitive Analysis                 • Structure & Function
                    MISSION            • Operational Strategy
            What the organization will • Quality Systems
            achieve at some point in   • Intellectual Capital
                  the future           • Change Management

                    CRITICAL SUCCESS FACTORS
                    • Critical Success Factors
                    • Preliminary Strategy Goals

MARKETING STRATEGY  DEPARTMENTAL STRATEGIES   HUMAN RESOURCES
• Marketing Mix     • Objectives              STRATEGY
• Application       • Operational Plan        • HR Admin Practices
                    • Departmental One-page Plan • Employee Development
                                               • Succession Planning

FINANCIAL STRATEGY  OPERATIONALIZING          INFORMATION TECH-
• Income Statement  THE STRATEGY              NOLOGY STRATEGY
• Capital Requirements • Critical Success Factors • IT Value Assessment
• Budgets           Consensus                 • Business Information
• Key Assumptions   • Finalize & Prioritize     Assessment
                      Strategic Goals         • Opportunity Assessment
                    • Resource Scoping

IMPLEMENTATION &    ONE-PAGE STRATEGIC
CONTROL             PLAN
• Implementation    • Vision, Mission & Core
• Reporting           Values
• Measurement & Control • Critical Success Factors
                    • Prioritized Goals &
                      Milestones
```

Figure 2

Celebrating Success!

- Detailed Action Plans linked to each goal
- Resource scoping plans that allow trade-offs of resources against priorities
- Rigorous documentation of the planning work sessions

The benefits of this process are seen in accelerating achievement since the team has:

- An expanded range of alternatives examined because many perspectives have been efficiently incorporated,
- Better tactics as the extended knowledge of many has been utilized, and
- Alignment around the actions and responsibilities through an iterative, collaborative planning process

Today, modern technology offers us some strong tools for developing solid strategic plans by achieving broad-based participation and building needed consensus, even in highly distributed or complex organizations. One such tool is web-based planning software. This can be combined with the guidance of senior experienced professionals in order to assist your team in effectively establishing a comprehensive plan to achieve your growth objectives. The software-enabled approach efficiently permits contributions across time zones and geography, and enables visibility of multiple inputs in order to allow discussions built on shared knowledge to produce strategies, tactics, tasks, metrics, and targets that are understood by all who will be responsible for implementation. Again, the objective is an approach that produces a plan that will be owned by the organization rather than a prescriptive plan developed by a few key members of management or by outsiders.

Business Strategy

Using a software-enabled process is not the only way and, where it is not feasible, the same process can be undertaken using "paper and pencil." When the size of the key management team is small, this is probably the most effective approach. With a larger team, it will probably result in a requirement for more time (especially in group meetings) and more meeting discipline to ensure time is not wasted. A good meeting facilitator (preferably one who is not part of the organizational staff) is an essential element here.

Making Business Strategy Part of your Everyday Business Activity

Most companies believe intellectually that some form of a formal business strategy is needed to guide operations and to assure good performance. Yet the majority of these companies will admit that their business strategy has failed to live up to expectations and to deliver promised results.

So what is the problem ?

In reality the problem is two-fold. First, many companies continue to use top-down, financially driven, tactically focused processes designed to run yesterday's organizations. Typically, goals are financial and internally focused, and do not get to the "whys" and "hows." Second, traditional business strategies are developed using the 'analysis and recommendation' model. In this model, the business strategy essentially pops out at the end of a one-time effort – usually developed by an outsider with limited input from key stakeholders. By the time the business strategy sees the light of day, so much money and time has been invested, that there is little opportunity for (or willingness to listen to) input by those who have to make it happen. Without this input, those charged with implementing that business strategy do not enjoy a

Celebrating Success!

sense of ownership in the plan, and flaws may go un-addressed. Neither approach has the flexibility to adjust to changes in the competitive landscape or in the marketplace.

There is a better way

Key thought shifts needed to move toward business strategy development that yields results include:

- Business strategy development is a process not an event
- Good execution is more important than good strategy
- Understanding and commitment are key to execution
- Executing the business strategy is everyone's everyday job
- Continuous monitoring is an essential element of a good business strategy
- Adjustments to the business strategy must be made at frequent intervals

This discussion leads to an important conclusion:

Your business strategy must be a process not an event.

Achieving an actionable plan to implement your business strategy requires participation that is broad but efficient; collaboration created by building on the best elements from many perspectives, experiences and capabilities; and consensus achieved through debate, dialog and resolution of differences. A process that incorporates these elements provides tactics and targets representing the best thinking of the business, and alignment around the goals, path, actions, and responsibilities. An alignment-driven business strategy planning process will be a new concept for some. Yet it can provide a comprehensive, efficient means to adjust varying viewpoints behind a single business strategy toward a common objective. Otherwise, even the best plan cannot be executed effectively.

Emphasize Execution

Even the best business strategy will not deliver results if it is not well executed. However, superb execution of a less-than-ideal business strategy will serve an organization very well. There are two aspects of execution that merit comment – both have to do with the "people" side of the ledger.

It's not enough just to create new tactics around marketing, sales, production and other key functions. "People" issues must be addressed. Competencies – the capabilities an organization must have to succeed – must be present and in the right positions. Giving an individual job goals, performance metrics, and incentives will not produce desired results if the individual lacks the competencies needed to accomplish their part of the business strategy. Sometimes dramatic changes in the business environment create large gaps between what is needed to do a job and the competencies resident within the individual charged with doing it. It is essential that such gaps be closed – through development, addition or replacement. Failure to close the gap when the job is essential to business strategy execution will sow the seeds for broader failure throughout the organization.

Behaviors are the second "people" factor that impacts an organization's performance. Ask yourself the question: "Do I ever see behaviors in the organization that are counterproductive to where we are taking the company?" If the answer is even close to a "yes" or "maybe," then the good news here is there are short-term actions that can be taken to address the issue. Ignoring it, on

Celebrating Success!

the other hand, means wasted time, resources, people and money – costs that few companies can afford in today's environment.

Organizations that incorporate behavioral change opportunities and incentives into their business strategies can realize substantial bottom-line benefits if they effectively define expectations and communicate them throughout the organization. By aligning behaviors with its strategic goals in a continuous improvement process, the company has the opportunity to gain significant sustainable strategic advantage over its competitors.

Develop Understanding and Commitment

An effective business strategy is well understood by the organization that must implement it and the organization is committed to the plan. Understanding and commitment are products of communications – and good communications take the form of a dialogue not a monologue.

Consistent, unambiguous communications up, down and across the organization are the lifeline of day-to-day execution. Studies have shown that one of the main reasons why companies do not successfully execute strategy is the lack of employee strategic awareness. Further, if managers put out different messages to their respective business units as to direction, priorities, and goals, redundancies, inefficiencies and errors will result. All detract from the bottom line.

Internal communications are an opportunity to reinforce key messages to the organization. Repetition of the same message by different people in authority is an effective means to not only ingrain the message into everyone's behavior but to underscore that the entire organization "is on the same page." There is strong evidence that when managers communicate well and employees understand goals, organizations perform well.

Make Executing the Strategy "Job One"

Business strategies that really work are totally infused into the company's day-to-day activity – they are not golden guidance delivered from on high. Ensuring that each and every employee understands how their activities impact the strategic plan goes a long way to ensuring that they will not act in a way that is counterproductive or unsupportive.

Continuous Monitoring is Essential

The dynamic, interconnected world we live in makes it mandatory that progress toward goals be measured frequently and adjustments made to accommodate changing conditions. Key customers may change direction unexpectedly, raw material supplies may be subject to price hikes or supply disruptions, and there is always the impact of world events that ripple through all sectors of the economy.

Keep Your Hand on the Steering Wheel

Your business strategies cannot remain static against such a backdrop. Therefore a key element of strategic plans must be a continual questioning of assumptions and measuring of progress. When gaps develop between what is happening and what was planned, changes must be made.

One of the best ways to prepare for developments outside the mainstream of assumptions is to build contingency plans into the strategy. Of course, even contingency plans need to be reviewed at the time they may be needed to assure continued validity. The point is to know about needed adjustments early and to make corrections

Celebrating Success!

in small increments. Waiting until things really get out of whack so that major adjustments are needed will destroy momentum and morale and deteriorate performance.

Summary

The essence of a successful business strategy is two-fold:

- Make your business strategy a part of the business' daily life.
- Develop the team along with the plan. The two cannot really be separated.

Failure to recognize these simple ideas has been the Achilles heel of business strategies for decades. In the final analysis, everyone in the company needs to understand how their job fits into the bigger picture and how that bigger picture plays to their individual interests. The synergies that result can carry a company a long way, even in a competitive environment and tough economy where frequent course corrections may be needed.

Developing an effective business strategy is not difficult – but it does require time and effort. There is no "right" approach – but you must be methodical, and getting some outside help to guide your team through the process can often be very beneficial and can improve your team's efficiency.

Most importantly, study after study has shown that businesses with well thought-out and clearly articulated business strategies that are part of the company's daily activity are regularly much more successful than their counterparts who lack such a business strategy.

Business Strategy

Questions for consideration:

1. Do you know where you want to go?
2. Do you have a plan for where you are going and how you are going to get there? Do you adjust it regularly to accommodate changes in the business environment?
3. Is your team on board? Do they understand and accept the goals, methods and skills required?
4. Are your skills and activities consistent with your goals?

By Charles M. Gilmore, Principal, Avantt Consulting

cgilmore@ avanttconsulting.com, 330-867-9860

Chapter 9
FINANCIAL AND BUDGET

A budget is simply a plan – a financial plan – which is written down and quantified. It is a part of the overall business plan. One major reason for a budget is to provide the firm with financial goals. If you have no plan, you have no idea of what you hope to achieve or even if you are moving in the right direction.

A primary purpose of a budget is to force management to think ahead. When plans are made in advance, more choices are available than when operating in firefighting mode. This is roadmap for better making decisions.

A final benefit of budgeting is that it becomes a tool for communication, and provides a corporate framework for standardizing activities and communicating goals. The CEO uses the budget process to show stakeholders (including staff) where he or she wants to take the organization.

The master budget is broken down into operating budget and financial budget. The operating budget provides all the information necessary to prepare a budgeted income statement. The financial budget includes the cash budget and financial projections.

Once the budget is created, it is helpful to have a budgeting process. Budgeting is the frequent comparison of actual and budgeted items. This allows an organization to investigate variances and to correct problems when it strays from our budget.

Celebrating Success!

The first step in the budgeting process is the completion of an environmental statement. The environmental statement allows the corporation to understand their position with their suppliers, competitors, and customers. This includes changes in customer base, technology changes, and industry trends. This lets the company know where there is room for improvement and how much they need to improve.

Management then develops a set of general objectives. This is a broad-based look at what the firm hopes to achieve. Is the company in rapid growth, facing pricing pressures, customer erosions, planning expansion or facing competitive pressure?

The next step in the budget process is developing a set of financial assumptions. This includes assumptions about inflation rate, impact of competitors on product prices and sales activities, potential price increases from suppliers, etc. After a clear understanding of the environment is defined, measurable goals should be established.

At this time I would like to discuss goal setting. Goals must be achievable, measurable and time bound. Achievable goals assume that they are realistic; 'stretch' goals are good, but goals that demand too much can create internal and external problems (see the chapter on Attitude).

Measurable assumes that they are being tracked and measured allowing for corrective action to be taken when variances are defined. Finally, a good goal is time bound. This means that a specific time frame is assigned for achieving a specific goal. The budgeting time frame is usually yearly.

There are many aspects of goal setting that are important and I would like to mention a few now. This is a quick review of chapter 6.

Financial and Budget

1. If you are dissatisfied with your company's performance, you need to make sure goals are identified, communicated and measured.
2. Make sure your corporate values allow you to support your goals. Goals need to be consistent with these corporate values. If you create goals that are not consistent with the corporate values (usually identified by a company's culture) you created an inherent conflict between what you want to accomplish and corporate expectations.
3. Prioritize your goals and fix your attention on the numbers on goals. The more goals you focus on the more difficult is becomes.
4. Make them measurable.
5. Create your plan and implement it.
6. Measure your progress and adjust accordingly.

If we look at conference participants, they reinforce these ideas with their comments:

"Spend money the right way."

"Making investments wisely – don't fear spending according to a plan."

"Know and measure the numbers. Measure and consider risk and reward."

"Manage the banks. We found that local community banks were not as supportive of small business as the large regional banks."

"Don't be under-funded. Stay focused!"

"And last but not least: Manage by the numbers and watch cash flow."

Celebrating Success!

Many of the conference presenters talked about the importance of using the numbers to take calculated risks (see section on Risk). By having a good handle on the numbers they are better able to identify opportunities that are consistent with their financial goals.

These same companies talked about making purchasing decisions that were planned. If a need new technology was planned for in the budget, there was a need identified and solutions sought?

As variations to plan were identified, were these variations due to an unforeseen change in the market, customer base, or pricing structure from supplier? Did this require an adjustment to the existing plan? If so what was the impact on the rest of the business?

Summary

The budget and planning process was very important to conference participants. This plan defined the existing financial environment, looked at external factors that could impact the company, allowed the company to developed goals and measures the progress against these goals. The process needs to be flexible enough to make changes based on variances and changes in the financial and business environments.

Questions for consideration:
1. Does your company have a financial budget in place?
2. If so, is it being used to make purchasing decisions?

Financial and Budget

3. Does the budget support the business's strategic plan?
4. When you create your financial plan do you take into consideration the behavior of your suppliers, competitors and customers?
5. Are the goals of your financial plan consistent the company's culture? For example, if a company growth has been flat for years, it might not make sense to set an aggressive target until you are sure the right people are in place and the marketing and sales organization can support this.

   It might not make sense to compete in price unless you have driven the cost out of the business that allows you to compete on price
6. Does your company have the tools to measure budget versus actual performance against plan?

Chapter 10
BUSINESS PROCESS IMPROVEMENT

Every company has processes; some are clearly defined, others are implicit. Business processes are the way a business does things. Each company that submitted nominations to last year's Greater Akron Business Conference talked about how there was a need to continuously improve existing business processes, to become more efficient, effective and productive while reducing costs.

Business Processes include a wide variety of tasks: processing invoices, servicing customers, shipping products, and handling complaints. Anything a business does involve a process in some way shape or form. It can be measured, modified, streamlined and redesigned (created).

How do you know what processes need improvement? Problems manifest themselves in different ways. Some examples of problems in business processes are below. Does the process have:

- Inherent delays
- Excessive transportation and storage requirements
- Low ownership and/or accountability
- High rework requirements
- Significant paper handling
- The same problems keep reappearing

Celebrating Success!

- High waste
- Poor feedback system
- Focus on quantity not quality
- Long cycle times/long process times

Many of the companies I talked with were very clear on the impact of implementing process improvement in their businesses.

"... putting a process in place that ensures that everyone is treated the same (especially important during growth)"

"Continuous improvement is essential, especially based on customer feedback."

"Constantly analyze and improve your business or production processes."

"The way to succeed is continuous improvement; nothing is sacred."

"When business processes are broken down into well-defined segments, individuals who may not have completed an advanced degree can become excellent employees."

"Put people first – have your hiring, education and termination processes firmly in place."

"... one secret is to carefully nurture the sales process with a unique approach: he uses an internal sales staff, but because different qualities are valuable in each of the stages of selling – generate/qualify/close ... he actually uses different people for each stage."

The business processes used in many businesses have not been designed, they have evolved over time. This leads to business

Business Process Improvement

processes that are not as effective and efficient as they could be. Many times activities occur that add no value to the outcome.

Many companies understand the value of process improvement from the financial perspective but not the overall implications. Business processes:

- Drive a company's culture
- Define how new employees are trained
- Set expectations on how customers are treated
- Propagate the attitude of the company owners throughout the organization.

The need to design a business process can occur for several reasons:

- Mergers or acquisitions
- Inefficiencies, cost control
- Lack of process effectiveness
- Competition and global pressures

One of the biggest opportunities that was made available when doing process improvement was to drive a specific set of behavioral expectations into an organization. **Processes drive behavior.** If you are not getting the desired results (behaviors) from your employees, good processes can address that.

You cannot manage outcomes, only behaviors. If you are not getting the results you expect, are you managing the behaviors that drive the desired results? Behaviors changes can be implemented through understanding the behavior you want from your employees, implementing the processes to drive that behavior and measuring the results.

Celebrating Success!

It is important to measure the results, otherwise how would you know how effective the process has become. Many people assume that once a business process is modified that the work is over. That's partially correct. A good process is not only measurable but time bound as well. As your business changes it becomes necessary to maintain the progress made by "enhancing" your processes.

If you don't do this, the ineffectiveness that created the need for change is reintroduced into the process.

Be careful not to become too internally focused on your business processes. Many companies see great results in designing or redesigning process and over time they spend more time working on the activities of process improvement instead of focusing on the expected results of the process.

One company I worked for refused to let a proposal go out the door until over 20 people reviewed it. In this process, people would fly in from all around the country for monthly configuration review meeting. People were more focused on the meeting then the result of the meeting. This resulted in the sales organization finding ways to circumvent the process in order to be more responsive to the client. In most cases the configurations being reviewed were not the same configurations being presented to the client.

If you are thinking about implementing a process improvement project in your company, a good methodology (overview) is especially important. The one I used is described below.

1. Planning & Organization – Know what you want the redesign to accomplish. For example, do you want to:

    • Drive out cost

Business Process Improvement

- Make the company more responsive
- Implement an empowering employee culture
- Clearly define roles and responsibilities

2. Data Gathering & Recording – What data do you need to gather? How do you gather that information? Will you do interviews, conduct employee surveys, document the existing process, or conduct site surveys? Know how the data gathering supports the project objectives.

3. Analyze Data – Take what you learned and create a baseline process. After the baseline is completed, you can better understand the implications of making a change in the process.

4. Create a Work Analysis Report – Document what you uncovered and distribute the results to the correct audience for validation and approval.

5. Redesign the Process – Redesign the process to drive the expected behaviors, cost saving, productivities, etc. defined in the Planning & Organization phase of the project.

6. Analyze Risks – Understand the risks associated with the planned changes. Do a risk analysis and create a contingency plan in the event certain risks materialize.

7. Create an Implementation Plan – Many times when processes are changed, companies use the opportunity to implement new technologies. Process improvement does not necessarily imply technology, but it is a reasonable expectation. When technology is implemented, make sure you know the best way to implement and utilize it effectively.

Celebrating Success!

8. Create a Cost/Benefit Analysis – The catch here is that the cost/benefit is listed last. In reality, there should be a review of expected costs and benefits with each phase of the project. This step is nothing more than the formalization of what you have learned in the prior steps.

Summary

In summary, poorly designed or implemented processes are the root cause of many problems.

- Most processes have not been designed.
- Well-designed business processes have a clear definition of roles, responsibilities, expected time frames and process objectives.
- Well-defined business processes can lead to improved employee morale, improved productivity, reduced costs and improve bottom-line performance.

Questions for consideration:

1. Do any of your processes require rework?
2. Do the same problems keep reoccurring?
3. Is there high waste?
4. Do your processes have poor feedback systems?
5. Is process cycle time too long?
6. How long are the process delays? Is this a problem?
7. Who owns the process? Who do you go to if the process is not working?
8. Are the people in the process being held accountable for the

Business Process Improvement

    quality of their work?

9. Does the process have clearly defined roles and responsibilities?

Chapter 11
INFORMATION TECHNOLOGY

I have been working in the information technology industry for over two decades. I have been though a lot and I have seen a lot. I find information technology to be a major asset to many companies. For some companies though, it is a source of major heartache.

An information technology that supports the business plan is an ideal way to manage and implement technology. It simplifies the purchasing of technology because you are buying for a reason, not because it is the latest and the fastest.

Implementing a full technology strategy can have a benefit that cascades throughout the organization. For example, one company I did work for was building their own PCs because they thought it was less expensive to do it this way. When we analyzed the true cost, it became apparent that this was not the case: the component cost was less expensive but we had higher costs in other areas.

For example, when a machine broke we needed to take it apart and send the broken component back to the vendor. The time to take the machine apart, the shortened warranties, the component cost of keeping extra parts and rebuilding the machine, when included in the total cost, made it clear that it was far less expensive to standardize on one vendor and buy those PCs.

Celebrating Success!

Another example was how a company purchased a software application. They assumed they could do it themselves less expensively then engaging an experienced consultant. Seven years later the application was still not installed correctly. They over estimated their skills, did not plan effectively, did not assign the correct resources to the appropriate activity and under funded the project.

On the other hand, when a technology strategy is defined and implemented, the risk is significantly reduced. The strategy needs to address:

- Company hardware and software standards
- Definition of roles and responsibilities
- Vendor performance management criteria
- Asset retirement strategy
- Buy versus lease analysis
- Support the business plan

It is clear from talking with most conference participants, Information Technology played an important role.

Fortney & Weygandt states so eloquently: "Focus on the function! Let the technology worry about itself as you focus on the needs of the customers – and make sure what you build is flexible enough to change with the market."

RADcom used an online sales forecasting tool to better understand what kind of customer base it had, how it was pricing its products and how to set its pricing structure.

Several of the companies involved in the conference were technology based companies: OnlyOne, Software Answers, OEConnection, AZTEK, Cardinal Commerce, Brulant, TimeWare,

Information Technology

ICBS, etc. They either sold technology-based solutions or use technology to solve business problems for themselves or their clients.

Having spent my career in the Information Technology industry, I have a unique view. Early in my career I was involved in automating people-intensive manual operations on large mainframe computers. Each application was written specifically for the department requesting it. The concept of packaged solutions did not yet exist.

During this time, one of the biggest costs was the hardware infrastructure: the mainframe computer, the computer room, raised floors, air conditioning, wiring, electrical, etc. At this point, it was less expensive to have many people support these applications than it was to have stronger infrastructure. Over the years, the opposite happened. The hardware cost dropped and the people became the largest costs. In the early 70's, a mainframe computer would cost millions. Today, I have more computing power in my Pocket PC then was available on the large mainframe computer of the time.

Because the price kept dropping, more and more companies were able to afford the costs associated with a technology purchase. This was reflected in how companies used technology to drive their business and service their clients.

Whole segments of the economy were created to address these new opportunities. Some examples follow:

- Customer resource management
- Enterprise resource management
- Financial forecasting
- Shop floor applications
- Sales force automation

Celebrating Success!

- Bill of material and inventory control

The conference participants that use technology are listed below with a brief description of how technology affected their business. This list is not meant to be a comprehensive description, or to reflect what a specific company does. Only the company itself can do that. My point here to stress that technology has woven its way into the daily lives of these companies and to amplify how deep this relationship is.

Please see the stories later in this document for more details and be sure to visit the web site for each company. You will learn far more about them then I can share here.

- OEConnection created its business model to serve the automotive aftermarket using technology.
- OnlyOne uses voice technologies to address a market need by combining different technologies into a cohesive solution.
- 5iTech takes various technologies developed in Russia for commercialization in the United States.
- Interactive Media Group uses computer code written under the "Open Source" umbrella and creates solutions for business problems.
- Fortney & Weygandt, Inc. developed a piece of software to help them streamline their business.
- Gateway Title Agency has a very good system for tracking titles in process. It lets the owner know the productivity of the business with the push of a button.
- Mustard Seed Market has automated a number of the business processes as it has grown.
- Continental Cuisine Eatery created a custom application

Information Technology

to run their cash registers and track the results of their business.

- Allergy & Respiratory Center built a customized solution to create a specific environment for the doctor's patients.
- Aztek is a technology company that provides excellent customer service.
- Bonnie Cohen Ceramic Design uses email and the Internet to run her business.
- Brulant is a technology company and understands the value of using technology to solve business problems for their clients.
- Cardinal Commerce uses technology to solve ecommerce business problems.
- DecisionPoint Marketing & Research created a dedicated lab to allow companies to evaluate how easy web applications are to use.
- Physicians Medical Service Bureau, Inc. uses technology to solve problems for its clients. It has allowed the owner to create the kind of life he wanted.
- RADcom, Inc., a technical writing and training firm, uses a web-based sales force automation tool to stay on top of the sales process.
- Software Answers, Inc. is a software development company that creates solutions for schools.
- Bright.net Internet Providers provides Internet access to home and business users.
- Foundation Software is a software technology company that provides solutions for the construction industry.
- Lazorpoint, Inc. is another technology company.
- MrExcel.com created an entire company around one of

Celebrating Success!

Microsoft's products, Excel.

- TimeWare Inc. uses technology to create time reporting applications for their clients.

- Unicall International Inc., a call center, uses technology tools to support the business.

- United Security Management Services, Inc. uses telephone technology to solve problems for their clients.

- ICBS, Inc. is a technology company that creates and manages web sites.

- NCS DataCom, Inc. is a technology company.

- Neighborhood Manufacturing, a Div. Of Superior Tool Co., uses the latest in technology tools to maintain competitiveness.

It has been my experience that many smaller companies do not effectively utilize technology because they do not understand it. This is not meant to be a criticism but more of a reflection of the resource constraints smaller companies face.

Smaller businesses are focused on what they do best, running their business. They typically do not have time to understand how the effective use of technology can help them drive out cost and improve productivity. For many companies, technology provided a way to position their company in a unique way. For others it truly is a competitive advantage.

Summary

Technology is here to stay. It's core to many of these companies and is used in every company to solve a variety of business problems.

Information Technology

Questions for consideration:

1. Does your business plan have a technology component?
2. Do you have a trusted technology advisor who can help you sort out what technology can work in your company?
3. Does the information technology installed in your company do what you need it to do?
4. Does your IT employee understand how to apply technology to solve your business problems?
5. Are you happy with your technology vendor's performance and customer service? If not what would you like to do about it?
6. Do you have & track software licenses for all users?
7. Have you implemented project management tools and techniques?
8. Does your company have a technology asset management program??
9. Do you know what percentage of revenue you spend on IT purchases as compared to your competition?

Chapter 12
MARKETING

Marketing played a critical role in the success of many of the companies that participated in the Greater Akron Business Conference. Here is what conference nominees and presenters had to say about marketing:

"Visit peers to learn from their success and failures."

"Don't be afraid to spend money to make your image more professional."

"Clients value having a complete marketing program and the ability to gauge results."

"Be flexible when evaluating the market and keep the big picture in sight."

"Capitalize on [your] signature strength by understanding [your] "crusade" and the emotions [your] customers go through in using [your] product/system."

"He differentiates himself from the competition by knowing who his customers are and building their trust. And he has cloned his system by taking his Excel crusade and building a story and a system around it."

"The key lies in sound customer-centered marketing strategy and your expertise and passion for what you do."

Celebrating Success!

"And make sure to leverage your product to create additional revenue streams from different applications, different markets."

"Growth came from word of mouth – not advertising."

"And always remember, "Clients don't care about what we think is important!""

"Watch carefully. Look for trends, listen to your customers and respond quickly. Most of all – care."

"Realized that as he built his reputation, he was not only selling the "ahs" but also selling "comfort" to his clients."

"It's as much about painting the visual picture to the client as it is about creating the "wow.""

"Proactive communication with clients ensures that expectations are exceeded."

There are as many definitions for marketing as there are marketers and companies. But when you get right down to it, perhaps the best way to define marketing is by its result: *becoming the obvious choice for your ideal customer.*

There are three primary components to becoming the obvious choice –

1. Your crusade. This is the soul and the personality behind what you do and how you do it. It's what makes your organization unique and distinctly different from any other provider. It's the story behind your business and the reason you're in business. Successful organizations don't underestimate the importance of their crusade because they know that their ideal customers recognize its value. It's this very soul behind the business that attracts their ideal customer and keeps them loyal regardless of price.

Marketing

2. Their desire. Your ideal customer is constantly scanning; both literally and figuratively. They are always looking for solutions that fit them perfectly. They are educating themselves using the Internet, using their friends and using other providers who come to them with offers. They are running partially on data and partially on "knowing what they want when they see it." Successful marketers know who their ideal customer is and have a structure that makes them recognizable as "The One".

3. The system. This is your product, service and the way your customer experiences doing business with you. Your system begins when you or information about your organization "touches" your customer. That's when their experience begins. Building your marketing system around helping your customer make good decisions or giving your customer the best experience with your product or service makes you hard to replace.

When you look just below the surface of products, pricing, promotions and distribution, marketing is visceral. It is all about understands the emotional nuances that our customers have to go through and endure to fill the gap that exists between what they have, what they want and what everyone out there is clamoring to offer.

Marketing is emotional. It's all about understanding the urgency our customers feel, the pain and frustration they endure and the salve our offering provides in the often cold, heartless, indifferent world of purchasing and consumption.

The academics call this buyer behavior. But it's so much more than that. Buyer behavior is a clinical term. But we all know that

Celebrating Success!

whether we're buying cars, casters or ball bearings, purchasing is an emotional process. The higher the investment, the higher the emotional involvement in the purchase is.

Here are a few ways to get at the root emotions that drive your customers' buying behavior. By simply understanding the emotional investment they make in their decision, you will be able to position your product or service in a way that will be most meaningful to them and address what they want most.

Exercises:

1. When does your customer start thinking about buying what you sell? What situation are they in? What evidence do they have that they need your product or service?

    Answering these questions will help you envision the specific circumstances that your customers are in when they start thinking about your product or service. In fact, if you put yourself in your customers' shoes, you may realize that they may NOT be thinking about your product or service when they should be. All of this is important. Write all of this down with as much visual detail and emotional content that you can. Be your customer. Watch your customer; look at their body language and tone of voice. Where is there frustration, how can your product or service help them.

2. What's important to your prospect when they are buying what you sell? You can start by listing the first things that come to mind i.e. results. But how much emotion is there in just results? *Anyone* can promise results and all of us do. That comes right on the heels of "solutions." Be specific and actually use the words your customer would use.

    If you were to think about what is important to you when you're buying a car you might say "I don't want to be

Marketing

sold" or if you were buying a drill you might say "I want the salesperson to be knowledgeable about carpentry." If you were looking at landscapers you might say "Come when you say you'll come. Send me a quote when I ask for one or show up when you say you will." You can see the different positioning possibilities any of these avenues can offer. In addition to that, all you would have to do is focus on one area that holds the highest emotional value to your customer and you will beat your competitors hands down.

3. What information does your customer need to make a decision? The law of pricing pressure is that people buy on price when they don't have anything else to compare. If your price is high, there's a good reason for it. Document those things and educate your customer as to what quantifiable value this has to them in the long run.

If you can simply get close enough to your customer to document what the little voice inside their head is saying about the sheer subject of your product or service, you will not only leapfrog your competition, you will become the master of your marketplace.

And when you think about it, that's the goal of any successful business. Marketing strategy and its supporting systems are nothing more than the processes that make that desire a reality.

We live in a buyer's economy. The advent of technology and high-speed information sharing has made the world a much smaller place and that has made it easy for us to become fairly savvy and smart consumers – especially when it comes to high-involvement, high-dollar purchases. Put simply, that means that the days of selling are over and the days of educating and informing and choosing are here.

Summary

Marketing is emotional – it is understanding what drives your customers' decisions, and how you can address their needs. Price is the lowest common denominator – if you can educate clients on what you can offer beyond price, you can win over the competition.

Questions for consideration:

1. Do you understand who your customers are and what they need? How are you going to find out?
2. Does your marketing tell your customer how you will address their needs, or does it tell them what a great widget you have?
3. What steps do your customers take when making their purchase decision? Where and how can you get their attention?

By Ivana Taylor, ThirdForce Marketing

330-472-0981

ivana@ thirdforce.net

Chapter 13
SALES

Our conference participants were not bashful in expressing the importance and impact of a well-designed sales methodology and approach.

Here is what conference nominees and presenters had to say about sales:

"Referrals are golden."

"Relationships and energy count for everything."

"Imagining – and then creating – win-win situations."

"Get to the sales fundamentals. Identify what is 'good business,' then pursue it relentlessly."

"Focusing on the fundamentals of the sales process 8 hours a day while doing it with measurable repeatable processes."

I've worked with thousands of salespeople in hundreds of companies over the years. The successful salespeople, entrepreneurs and business owners have the following traits in common. First, they set goals; they have a clear vision of what and where they want to go. Many entrepreneurs have a dream but not detailed plans or a roadmap for their journey.

Goal setting is putting your dreams into a written plan. The plan includes benchmarks with dates for tasks to be completed. Those successful people also do something that's interesting. They

Celebrating Success!

develop backup contingency plans. When they hit a roadblock, they're ready with plan B. In other words, they anticipate hurdles that are sure to emerge along the way and they have a backup plan or strategy in place to deal with them before they smack right into them.

One of the other keys is to know your limitations and accept them. The successful people I've worked with were not afraid to ask for help and they didn't try to do everything themselves. One of the biggest mistakes you can make is thinking that you can do everything without help. Ask yourself, "is this task worthy of my time", or "could someone else do it quicker and less expensively than I can?" Spend your time on issues that play to your talents and strengths. And remember early on in your development or in your business, sales needs to come first. All too often, I find that sales people, entrepreneurs and business owners spend a lot of time getting ready and getting a lot of technical stuff out of the way but they don't remember that nothing happens until someone sells something.

I subscribe to the S.M.A.R.T. acronym for goals.

Specific: State goals very specifically.

- i.e. "I want to sell ten units of widgets by November 30th of this year with a margin of thirty percent or more."

Measurable: Your goal statement must contain a method of measuring your progress (years, age, date, time, place).

Achievable: You have to believe that you can achieve your goal. It must have reasonableness to it.

- If you are 60 and set a goal to climb Mt. Everest, it may be unreasonable.

Sales

Relevant: Your goal must be your goal, not what someone else desires for you. If it is not your goal, you will have no passion for it.

Time Specific: Your goal must have a definite starting point and a stated completion date.

Referral-Based Marketing

Marketing is a logical next step that is closely tied to goal setting. Without clear goals, you cannot develop a viable marketing plan.

Word of mouth, referral marketing or referral-based marketing, as I like to call it, is one of my favorite methods for promoting many businesses. Referral based marketing must be focused to be successful.

Prospects obtained from referrals will allow you to:

1. Focus your efforts. You will be focusing your efforts on prospects that know what you sell, have a need or want for what you sell, and would like to discuss it with you, and they have been referred to you by someone they admire, respect and trust. This takes a lot of the deception and rejection out of the buyer/seller dance.

2. Build trust quickly. Referrals allow you to build trust quickly because some of the relationship that the referrer had with your referral source transferred to you. The referrer normally will speak very highly of you, your professional expertise, and/or your character. This allows you to build trust quickly and effectively with prospects. We have to remember that people do business with people they like and trust.

3. Get to their needs quickly. One of the important steps of being successful in sales is to get prospects, clients and

Celebrating Success!

customers to share their needs with you and to share their personal thoughts and feelings. Referrals allow you to accomplish this much quicker and more effectively because you've come highly recommended, they understand why you're there and they value what you bring to the table. Rather than being seen as just another peddler, you've positioned yourself as a true problem-solver and consultant and they willingly share their true needs and true wants with you.

4. Make a good impression early. Edification seems to be a dying art today. If you teach your referral sources how to edify you; in other words, speak well of your character, who you are as an individual, you will find that the sales process moves along much quicker. Because you have been positioned not only as someone with a product or service that the prospect could use but you've also been positioned as a kind of person, even if they don't do business with you, they would like to meet.

5. Encourage a customer service orientation within your business. Think of the referrer as the goose that lays the golden egg and the referrals as the golden egg. Because you value the golden eggs, and hopefully the goose that lays them, you will find yourself gravitating to more of a customer service orientation within your company. By not spending thousands of dollars on direct marketing campaigns, or hours cold calling, canvassing and prospecting, you can actually spend time servicing your client or customer base.

If you value the referral source, you want to make sure that any client or customer that you get from a referral source is given 110 percent in terms of quality, service and attention. One of the best ways to kill a goose that lays golden eggs

Sales

is not to take care of one of those golden eggs. Remember, they have a relationship with the person they referred to you. Your referrer's reputation is at risk if you drop the ball and don't follow through.

6. Reduce your non-productive sales activity. I have taught hundreds and hundreds of salespeople how to cold call and yet, in my opinion, it is the least effective method of obtaining prospects and marketing yourself or your company that there is. Am I suggesting that you never do a seminar, that you never make a cold call, that you never do a free talk to a community group such as Kiwanis, Rotary or the local business Chamber?; no. What I am suggesting is that as you become a referral-driven business you will find the need to do many traditional "sales" activities greatly diminished. I believe in having many legs on your marketing table, with referrals being one of them. I have just chosen to build my business primarily through referrals. I still do talks and I still do seminars, but in much lower numbers.

7. Increase your enjoyment of the sales and marketing function. You'll be in front of a steady stream of people and companies that want and need what you are selling and want to talk to you about what you have to offer.

For a moment I would like you to close your eyes and imagine that every week you are going out on two or three sales calls and you're going to be meeting with people that you've been referred to. They know what you do, someone has spoken highly of you and they're really looking forward to talking to you. Imagine that every month you were in front of three to five ideal prospects: they use a lot of your goods and services; they understand the value that a professional such as yourself brings to the marketplace; and

Celebrating Success!

they're willing to pay a fair price for that service or product. How much more time would you have, how much more fun would you have professionally and how much more financially rewarding would your sales career or business be?

To make this happen, you need to develop an ideal client profile. This would be a great time to grab a piece of paper and start writing as you go through this section. Write down everything you can think of to describe your ideal client or customer. Include such things as:

1. The dollar amount of sales to this client over the course of a year. If you're just starting out, think of what you want this ideal client to be and let's create it.

2. Products or services that they will use. When you look at your value proposition, in other words, when you look at all the goods and services that your company sells, or the ones that you really like to deliver because of margins, production capability, etc. how many of these goods and services will an ideal client utilize? Normally, ideal clients will utilize more than one of our products or services, unless of course, we only offer one product or service.

3. The typical wants or needs of your ideal client. This may require you to go and visit some of your ideal clients and to quiz them a little bit. Who are the individuals that will be using your product or service? We have economic buyers within a company but we also have end users. Who are the people that your product and service has an impact on within a company (or a household if selling to individuals)?

4. Decision-making. Who makes the decision and what is the decision making process that they go through?

5. Financial, social, demographic description. If a company, describe it in detail: annual sales, years in business, number

of employees, industry, market segments they service. Is it a single location or do they have multiple branches and locations? Are the decisions made at the corporate offices or are they made at the branch offices? If an individual, what are their assets? What are their age, occupation, marital status, are they male or female, net worth, is geography important? These are short lists, and I'm sure you can think of many other items you may wish to include here.

6. Environment. What "conditions" create a sense of urgency to move forward and act and what is the decision making process to act now? This becomes extremely important in helping referral sources recognize who they should refer to you and will become extremely important in knowing what questions to ask during the sales process.

I'm sure you can think of other areas to add to this list as you begin to work through this process. This is a process, it is ongoing and it is ever-changing. Your business will grow and change, and so will your ideal client and customer. And as we have all noticed, we are living in a period of extremely rapid change in business and the markets we serve. We either pick up on trends quickly and position ourselves or we get left behind. This is a document that I would suggest you revisit at least quarterly to make sure that nothing major has changed in what you would like an ideal client profile to look like.

Once you have defined what an ideal client/customer looks like, you can begin to focus your energy in that direction. Just as important, you can now focus your referral sources so that they are only presenting you with referrals that match your ideal client profile. If you can't articulate a clear concise message or description of what an ideal prospect looks like, sounds like or

Celebrating Success!

feels like, how can anyone help you get what you really want? Otherwise, you will have to sort through a lot of cats and dogs and deal with the frustration and rejection of cold calling and other more traditional forms of prospecting. A good resource is www.referraldoctor.com.

Selling

Ok, you now have clear concise goals and a written plan with completion dates and benchmarks to track your success and keep you moving in the right direction. You have created a referral based marketing plan. The next component is a selling system.

Successful salespeople are not born; they are created through hard work, study and following a proven-successful selling methodology. Most great salespeople have a sales coach or mentor and all have a selling system. Think of selling as a game. It has rules, it has regulations and the top performers in this game of selling all have a sales coach or mentor. It always amazes me why people think selling is so easy, and that all you need to do is be a great talker, jump up and down like a trained seal and people are going to stand in line to do business with you. Unfortunately, that is the stereotypical salesperson; fortunately that's not what the great ones look like.

Having a selling system that you follow religiously is probably more important than whose system you follow. There are a lot of great systems out there some of which may have been created just for your industry, product or service.

Without a selling system that has formalized and written steps on 'what, when and how' well defined, how do you figure where you are in the selling cycle or process? How do you know where you are in the buyer/seller dance? How do you duplicate success

Sales

and avoid failure? How can you analyze sales that are in process and determine the logical next step or do a postmortem on what could have been a great deal that got away if you don't have a system to rely upon and to use as a template?

Many times companies will hire me to help their salespeople with a particular need such as close more business. "Just teach my people how to close", is what they say. Upon further investigation, I many times find that their salespeople do an okay job of closing – when they are in front of a qualified prospect. The real problem, many times, is that their salespeople do not know how to qualify or disqualify an opportunity. So they have no choice but to treat every prospect the same.

Because these companies have not taken a systematic approach to sales, in other words, they do not have a clearly defined selling process or system, management is unable to really figure out where the real problem is. Is it a prospecting problem, is it a problem of knowing how to qualify and disqualify which opportunities to focus on, or is it a case of too much or too little of some behaviors? Because they have no system, they probably will never know.

Do you have a process or selling system that you religiously follow? Do you have a system to help you qualify and disqualify prospects and determine who is worthy of your time, effort and knowledge and who is not?

Many companies, because they do not have a selling system, don't know what's working for them and what is not because there is little or no consistency to their sales approach. In an effort to fix this, many times they decide to go the route of sales automation or what is often referred to as CRM. Management is then dismayed when the whole sales automaton or CRM project is a huge failure

Celebrating Success!

or the sales team refuses to use it. How do you put in a sales automation system when you do not have a selling system? A question worth contemplating, if you or your company is moving in this direction. Be careful or you might end up with automated chaos.

Great salespeople tend to have certain traits that I've observed over the years:

1. They believe in themselves. The really great ones are internally motivated, they have high self-esteem, they expect to win and they do win. They also have the ability to separate rejection of their product or service and rejection of themselves personally. In other words, they are able to separate who they are as individuals from what they do for a living.

2. They follow a selling system or process and learn how to identify where they are within that process or system. Great salespeople have built consistency and repeatability into how they go to market, how they work with prospects, clients and customers. This is one of the reasons they get consistent, predictable results.

3. They build trust and bond with prospects quickly. They understand the concept that people do business with people they like and trust. They adapt their behavioral style to fit the prospect and the situation. If you do not know what your behavior style is and how prospects and others perceive you, a good investment would be to take a quality behavioral, not personality, assessment. If you e-mail me at john@bothwellgroup.com, I will be happy to suggest a couple of behavioral assessments that are relatively inexpensive but extremely effective. I am of the opinion that prospects should see the salesperson that they need to

Sales

see, experience the salesperson they need to experience to do business. You can be you on your own time. On the sales call, you need to be whoever the prospect needs you to be.

4. They are good at asking questions and discovering prospects' needs and wants. Unsuccessful salespeople love to talk a lot, especially about themselves, their products and their services, but they spend very little time asking the prospect probing questions and discovering the wants and needs of the prospect.

5. They tend to be enthusiastic about their product or service. In other words, they are true believers in their product or service and you can tell they have conviction. When I say they are enthusiastic, I don't mean they are jumping up and down, saying how great their product or service is, or that they're overly emotionally involved in the sale. What I'm saying is, they're enthusiastic about the benefits of their product or service and they have conviction that what they have is of value and can help the prospect.

6. They are big-picture thinkers and don't get bogged down in minutia. There is a time to dot the i's and cross the t's in the sales process. Covering too much detail and giving prospects too many options turns the entire sales presentation or process into such a complicated jumble of this's and that's that it is almost impossible for a prospect to make a decision. In other words, they stay big picture and only hone in on those details that are germane to the conversation and that the prospect needs to know to make an intelligent, informed decision.

7. They tend to offer solutions later in the selling process than their less-successful counterparts. The successful salespeople offer solutions only after they have fully

Celebrating Success!

identified the problem and discovered what the prospect wants and needs. As a result, the successful salesperson is offering solutions to problems instead of offering features and benefits, which may or may not meet the needs or wants of the prospect.

8. They find out what the implication or impact of the problem or problems are on the company and the individual or individuals involved in the decision-making process. Remember, in many selling situations, we have economic buyers; they have one set of problems and needs and wants and we have end users that are part of that decision making process that have their own unique needs, wants and desires. Successful salespeople identify these and sell to them.

9. Only after building value for their solutions should they discuss money. And they've learned how to help the prospect build a budget by looking at the implications of the problems that the prospect is experiencing and what the return on investment will be based on the solutions that they are recommending to the prospect. If I hear it once a week, I hear it ten times a week, "but they have no budget." It is not unusual for companies and individuals not to have a line item budget for your goods and services. It is your job to help them discover that they have needs and wants and help them discover how much it is costing them in time and frustration not to have you as part of their business life. This is building value.

This is also the key to competing in the global economy. Potential customers may be able to get something cheaper overseas, but that also means that they may not be dealing with you and me. You need to become part of the value proposition that your clients and customers buy. Study after study has shown that one of the reasons that top salespeople are top salespeople is that their clients, their customers perceive them as individuals bringing value to the transaction.

10. When they present, they have a clear understanding of the prospect's needs, wants and desires, their budget and how the buying decision will be made. If you are not doing this, just know that you will probably be fifty to sixty percent less successful than your better-trained and better-coached competitor.

11. They understand sales is a game, I repeat, "sales is a game." They keep it fun and they know they can't get a hit every time at bat. They also know that they will also miss every ball that they don't swing at. The important thing is they are at bat and they decide which balls they are going to swing at and which balls they are going to let pass. They also know that to be really good at the game, they need to practice, they need to study and they need a batting coach.

12. When they don't hit the ball at a minimum, they get a lessons learned. By lessons learned, I mean that they learn a lesson. Spending a lot of time on a sale or on a project and not getting the business is ok if they've learned a lesson from it. Let's face it, education comes with a price. They do not take the loss personally, they analyze it, see what they could have done differently so the next time they're in this situation they're ready.

In closing, really great salespeople understand the value of having a coach. They utilize a systematic approach to sales, they are big picture thinkers, they are optimists by nature and they're trusting. They are also realists and they understand when to cut their losses and they always have a backup plan. They don't let

Celebrating Success!

their victories linger too long nor do they let their defeats linger too long. Great salespeople live in the moment. They are focused on the customer, the prospect that they're with right now. They're not thinking about tomorrow's sales, they're not worrying about the deal that got away; they live in the moment.

There's an old saying that if you chase two monkeys, both will get away. Those of you that like to quail hunt, one of the lessons you learn is if you chase the covey, you'll never get a bird. You pick one bird out of the covey, you follow it and you pull the trigger. Professional sales is going to the bank. It is picking one bird, one prospect, one client out of the covey. It's focusing on that client or customer, pulling the trigger, closing the sale or closing the file. A good resource for salespeople is www.bothwellgroup.com. Log on and sign up for their sales thought of the week and peruse their website which is full of tips and ideas.

Summary

Referral-based marketing offers some clear benefits over traditional, cold-call based sales. Knowing who your referrers are and what your "ideal" client is are keys to successful referral marketing. Sales processes need to be clearly outlined and weaknesses identified. Good salespeople are well trained, well prepared, and able to take risks

Questions for consideration:
1. Do you have clear, measurable, written goals? Are they SMART?
2. Are there referrers you should be using to reach out to

Sales

prospects? Who are they, and what do you need to do to reach out to them?

3. Do you know who your prospects should be? Can you write down their characteristics and target them?
4. Are you getting consistent, repeatable results from your sales staff?
5. Where is the problem in your sales process? Is it closing, or is it qualifying? Both?
6. What can technology really offer to improve your process?
7. Is your sales staff trained to put the customer first? Do they know how to evaluate their contacts and respond to customer needs and wants?

By John M. Bothwell Ph.D.

The Bothwell Group, Inc.

440-356-8774

jmb@bothwellgroup.com

Chapter 14
TRAINING

The biggest surprise for me in this entire project was the different views that conference participants held about training.

I heard stories of how training was used to:

- Create a company culture
- Drive cost out of the business
- Define roles and responsibilities
- Improve productivity
- Allow employees to make a greater contribution to the organization

According to the Greater Akron Chamber, the Tri-County area in Northeast Ohio (Summit, Medina and Portage) is the acknowledged center of the polymer industry; it is also the home of many of the country's most important manufacturers in such diverse fields as aerospace, nuclear power, automotive, construction, metals, machinery, plastics and chemicals. An uncommon variety of intricately engineered products, ranging from boilers for nuclear reactors and electronic circuitry to industrial valves and complex biomedical equipment, are produced in the three counties.

The region has also earned wide recognition for its capabilities in research and service-type enterprises. More than 80 percent of all academic polymer research is being conducted in Akron, and the University of Akron's Institute of Polymer Science is

Celebrating Success!

world acclaimed. Research and development work is also being conducted in such fields as cancer elimination, nuclear power, liquid crystals and biomedical engineering.

Approximately 300 metalworking firms provide support services for the area's manufacturing companies and provide employment for hundreds of technicians.

Insurance, chemical and retail companies have established division offices and warehousing in this strategically located area.

These, and other technical, white collar and service occupations, are expected to provide a large share of new jobs in the future. The wide diversity and blend of industrial-commercial, retail-distribution, service, and research operations provide the community with a cushion of self-sufficiency against national economic reversals and assures Tri-County residents of a continued healthy economy.

In order to keep up with these changes, our workforce needs to continue to improve the educational level of current and prospective employees. According to a recent study printed by the Greater Akron Chamber of Commerce, the age of tri-county area of Summit, Portage and Medina counties breaks down as follows:

Age	Percentage
Under 5	7.0%
5 - 17	18.1
18 - 20	5.2
21 - 24	6.1
25 - 44	31.9
45 - 54	10.4
55 - 64	9.0
65 & over	12.4%

Median age of population: 32.5

Training

In this same study, the Chamber discusses the educational attainment of the area.

Educational Attainment

Persons 25 years and over	497,130	
Less than 9th grade	29,508	5.9%
9th to 12th grade	74,247	14.9%
High school grad only	273,571	55.0%
Associate degree only	25,010	5.9%
Bachelor's degree only	64,477	13.0%
Grad or professional degree	30,317	6.1%

How is this significant? Fifty-five percent of the local workforce has only a high school education. In today's high tech world, where computers are a common business tool, it is safe to assume the local work force is going to need training as the market changes.

So how can we address this disparity between education levels that exist and the need for a highly skilled and technologically adept workforce?

Training

According to an International Study conducted by Coopers & Lybrands 1996, companies who conduct training gave the following reasons:

- Productivity increases
- Greater workforce flexibility
- Saving on material and capital cost
- More motivated workforce
- Improved quality of final product or service

Celebrating Success!

study indicates that training is most valuable when the business strategy, when outcomes are clear, and when training needs are supported by good HR practices.

Many companies that conduct training and are effective at linking training to a specific business strategy, implement business processes to reinforce training and create a company culture that advocates training.

This training does not always take place in a traditional classroom setting. It sometimes includes restructuring the business process to utilize an individual's strengths, allowing them to build on existing skills. This allows otherwise marginal employees to fit in and make a valuable contribution. There is web-based training, situational based training, and self-training.

The workforce is changing, the markets are changing and the general population has access to more information then ever before. Continued personally and professional development is needed. Each of us must understand that continued improvement of our existing skills and acquisition of new skills is critical.

Companies that understand this environment of continuous learning can contribute to the effectiveness of the organization and impact the bottom line.

Summary

Education, to be the most valuable, must be linked to the business strategy, have clear outcomes and be supported by good HR practices. Changes in the regional (and global) economy will require a more skilled workforce.

Training

Questions for consideration:

1. Does your company have a training plan in place that is structured to support the business strategy?
2. Is training measured to determine the financial and productivity impact to the organization?
3. How do you measure the impact of training in your organization?
4. Are your employees motivated to keep their skills current? If not, why not?

Chapter 15
GENERAL ADVICE

When I interviewed conference participants and reread the interview note, I wondered where to put some important information that I received. It did not seem to fit in any specific area of the book. Much of it could have been placed in any one of the 13 other categories, but that didn't seem to be appropriate.

There were too many nuggets of advice that made so much sense. I felt compelled to include them. I am not going to say much about them because they are self-explanatory. In many respects they are common sense. Sometimes we get so caught up in the day-to-day activities that we forget these simple concepts.

"Treat time as a precious commodity, because it is easy to get involved and let the business suffer."

"You can't try to solve too much too soon. Concepts need to be proven to solve real problems."

"Control the growth."

"I was surprised by how difficult it is to change behavior."

"When things get busy, don't work in the business, work on the business."

"Work hard and be honest with yourself and with others."

"Be resilient – it's essential to success. Be willing to change based on what you discover."

Celebrating Success!

"We didn't even consider failing on the promises we'd made."

"Keep the dream alive."

"You must really believe in your product and service and in your ability to deliver it to those who need it."

"Then work smarter *and* harder."

Chapter 16
BRINGING IT ALL TOGETHER

You read about all the different possibilities in moving your company forward. It can be confusing. So where do you start?

There are three attributes that are critical to becoming more successful. These are the three I consider to be the most important. The first is attitude, the second is business strategy and the third is focus.

Let look at attitude first. Conference participates were willing to put aside ego and engage the advice of quality advisors. They understood they could not be an expert in all fields. They sought out expert advice and trusted that advice. They implemented behaviors that were necessary for their success. They were willing to make the tough decisions and execute on those decisions.

If I had to be specific and tell you what I believe to the most important part of attitude, that would have the biggest impact on your business, it would have to be goal setting. Nearly every section of this book, in one way or the other, discusses the importance of proper goal setting. Reread the section on Attitude and Sales. Comprehend and internalize the discussion on goal setting.

As I apply the lessons in this book to my own life, I find that attitude is the most important for me. I find it essential to surround myself with a positive environment. I do this by reading positive and motivation material and listening to educational tapes and

Celebrating Success!

CDs. I associate with people who have a positive can do attitude and are willing to share their experience and expertise.

I am careful about what I read, who I associate with and what I think about. I am firm believer that what I think about is what I attract and create in my life. As a result, I focus on my goals, reframe less than positive experiences into positive learning experiences and I am not bashful in asking for feedback from my coaches and advisors. Because it is not possible to be an expert in everything, I utilize my coaches to help me and I listen to them.

Before I move forward, I need to spend time understanding what I want: feel what it's like to be successful, see myself as successful, create in my mind the exact situations I want to create in my life. If you cannot see it in my mind, I cannot create it in my life.

The single most important piece of advice I can give you is: do something! Don't wait for it to be perfect. It will never be perfect. Only action will take you when you want to be. Just get started!

The second step is to build a business plan. Don't over think the plan. Use it to get focused, provide clarity and direction to your pursuit. This will help you understand your market, how your product (or service) can solve specific problems, while providing clarity for your unique selling proposition.

Use this plan to focus your efforts. Before you take any action ask yourself "is this in my business plan and will it get me closer to my goal?" If the answer is no, then why do it. If it has to be done, move it lower on the priority list.

Your business plan is your roadmap into the future. A good plan will tell you where to spend your time, how to spend your time and

Bringing It All Together

provide clarity on the types of activities and opportunities that are most important to you. Your business plan is a living document. This plan allows you to recognize and capitalize on opportunities as they become available.

Remember, a great business plan that sits on the shelf is useless. A marginal business plan that is well executed will take you a long way towards your ultimate goal.

Finally, get focused! If you focus on the execution of your business plan, you will be clear on what is important. You will know when it is time to refuse business. You will have the ability to better identity the risks in a given opportunity. You will know when to engage referral partners and when to do it yourself.

Without the plan, one of the biggest problems we face is scattering of our resources. You can only focus on and do one or two things well at any given point in time. Your plan should clearly identify what those activities are. Be clear on what you want, be focused on what you want and be disciplined in staying on course.

After you address your attitude, create your business plan, and focus your efforts, you will find that you addressed all the other attributes in this book. Spend your time on your attitude, with special attention to goal setting, create your plan and stay focused. Know what is important and let the other "stuff" take a back seat.

Good luck to you and know that you can do it. Learn from the mistakes of others. Have fun and enjoy the journey!

Chapter 17
CONFERENCE STORIES

ALLERGY AND RESPIRATORY CENTER
Health Care

Dr. Given credits success of the Allergy and Respiratory Center to the concept of Kaizen, a Japanese term for continuous gradual improvement in work processes, and a visit to Disney World fifteen years ago. "My children enjoyed the rides and the Disney characters. I appreciated how investment, planning and careful execution could result in such a high level of efficiency and professionalism of the entire customer experience." From that point began the practice of weekly office meetings with both business staff and patient care personnel. In an atmosphere of mutual respect, they focus on providing quality patient care and respect, managing each step of the patient experience from the time the patient walks into the office until the time he or she leaves. A sampling of these steps include filling out forms, telephone contacts, payment arrangements, medical interview process, medical education, patient communication techniques, medical record keeping, prescription writing and scheduling appointments. "Through the analysis process, improvements can come in a number of ways – first, a step in the process may be no longer necessary, second, it could be done better, third, it could be done more easily, forth, it could be done by another worker, thus freeing a higher paid or more skilled worker to focus elsewhere or

Celebrating Success!

fifth, it could be a process that may lend itself to automation. By continuously reviewing our processes, we find improvements in all these levels," says Given.

Patient care is quite different in his office. The entire office works on a Microsoft Windows NT network and utilizes a computerized medical program to create, store and retrieve patient medical records. Each nurse works from his or her own exam room equipped with PC workstation and printer. "In the field of allergy, there is a need for a lot of discussion between care giver and patient. We know that it is important to spend as much time as needed with each patient and yet, for me to do that by myself with every patient is just impossible." Their response has been to invest in a high level of training for nurses. Equipped with this knowledge, technology and support, the nurses perform much of the interview and education processes. Dr. Given and his Nurse Practitioner are then able to focus on those elements of the evaluation - physical examination, clarification of diagnosis and treatment issues, prescribing of medications and whatever else may require their special skills or knowledge. An approach seems to be working "Everyone seems to win with this approach Patients appreciate the unhurried atmosphere and the emphasis on listening and explaining, nurses enjoy the face to face time with the patient and Joe (Nurse Practitioner) and I enjoy the role of teacher and supervisor" says Given.

"We began working on this in 1996 when there were no electronic medical records! We were flying by the seat of our pants but it was fun! It was very costly but the result has been a program that really fits our needs and our style of practice." Given points out benefits to automation of medical records such as reduced cost of medical transcription, reduced needs for storage of paper charts, reduced errors and improved overall efficiency.

Asked for advice, Dr. Given answers "There is no one rule but some points that have proven helpful to us are to determine what makes your product or service unique or superior. Hire as many smart people as you can afford. Constantly analyze and improve your business or production processes. Share knowledge with employees and encourage them to move up their levels of responsibilities. Look for applicants with a good attitude, natural intelligence and a willingness to learn. When business processes are broken down into well-defined segments, individuals who may not have completed an advanced degree can become excellent employees.

Dr. Given considers himself very fortunate. "I'm happy to have a job I love and people with whom to share it."

AZTEK
Marketing Communication - Web Site Design

Launched in 1997, Aztek never experienced a decline in business numbers even when others were going out of business. Because of the change in the business climate, however, and because customers were asking Aztek to do things outside the normal aspects of the business, the company realized there was a need to refocus. They analyzed what they were doing right and then moved into the market communications side of the business because "customers pushed them there."

To accomplish this, they hired key individuals – a total of eight added – who could help them move forward into the desired

Celebrating Success!

areas, allowing people to focus by reducing multitasking. They developed an account service team to focus on customer related issues, expanded the sales organization, and added personnel to the design team and the I.T. side of the business. They also relocated offices into an environment that better reflected the culture they were trying to create.

Aztek has learned to focus on core competency, but to be all things to all people using strong relationships – all clients are important and need to be treated the same. Aztek points out that having a variety of customers in many industries keeps the ideas fresh. The results have been outstanding in completion rates, dynamic/application based solutions, up time on hosting, quarterly goals exceeded every quarter in 2002, and a revenue growth of 22%-37% in the past three years.

Kevin Latchford, Director of Sales, stresses the importance of strong customer service, "Never close a door on a relationship." All design and development is done by full time employees so the customer has many points of contact with all people within the company. All customer questions are answered by the person who is responsible for the issues. Aztek has plans in place to expand their Northeast Ohio presence to Baltimore and Cincinnati over the next six months.

BONNIE COHEN CERAMIC DESIGN
Ceramic Tile & Creative Design for Endowment & Fund Raising

Bonnie Cohen is a designer and fine artist who creates decorative ceramic sculptures and handmade tiles that are sold in galleries and museums. Even though her work was featured in several

Conference Stories

national publications and sold well in galleries, Cohen wanted to expand her business to include large commercial installations and corporate commissions.

Technology provided the key element to expanding by opening up a whole new market for her designs. It started with the development of her website. Linking to and from several other larger websites, Cohen's site generated national inquiries about her work and within one year; she had obtained four large commissions to design donor recognition and fund raising walls. She uses e-mail, digital photography and conference calling to create and revise design details for these projects. For example, Cohen is currently working on a commission for the Jewish Seniors Agency of Rhode Island with the architect in Washington, D.C., the interior designer in New Hampshire and the signage company (doing the installation) in Maine. In Cohen's words, "Five years ago, I would never have dreamed of working on a project of this caliber from my studio in Akron, Ohio." Even though she may be hundreds of miles away, she can allow the client to "virtually" visit her studio every day to see how their project is coming along, ensuring the personal touch and passion she brings to the work.

Cohen has learned that it is important to balance your personal goals and others expectations. Her advice to other businesspersons includes: don't be afraid to hire the best help. Stick to what you do best and what you are passionate about, don't be afraid to spend money to make your image more professional, and don't let criticism get you down.

Celebrating Success!

BRIGHT.NET
Innovation and Reaching Out

It's not unusual in the software business to discover the product you need doesn't exist – and then write it yourself anyway. John Clarke, General Manager, found of Bright.net, made the most of it when his creative challenge came along.

Since taking care of 20,000 Internet Service Provider customers is no small responsibility, Alex and his team realized they needed serious protection against hacking and attacking. Being unable to locate anything that fit their unique needs as an ISP, they created one and called i-Trap. Turned out they weren't the only ISPs in the country who needed that kind of security.

But it wasn't just protection the i-Trap solution offered. The methodology Alex and his team created offers automated functionality that saves staff from having to monitor reports and screen out false alarms. It lets users access network traffic logs so they know where to start looking for intrusions. And with the highly detailed reports available, areas of the network that had never before been accessible were open to scrutiny, so improvements in performance became possible. For the first time, ISPs could afford to outsource intrusion protection without giving up control.

Not content to sell locally, Bright.net folks decided to "get more feet on the street" by creating a completely new DBA for the dealer channel that's now taking them into the national market.

Advice to entrepreneurs: Focus on the function! Let the technology worry about itself as you focus on the needs of the customers – and make sure what you build is flexible enough to change with the market.

Conference Stories

BRULANT
Profitability

It was a mistake, though not immediately obvious. As soon as Len Pagon realized that the partnership he'd formed was disastrous to the health of his digital strategy and consulting business Brulant, he cut his losses immediately.

After dissolving the partnership, Len and his team set out to re-align costs with expenses. In the face of a sagging economy with no relief in sight, they decided to position the company as a regional leader and pay close attention to sales from existing relationships. First steps included recreating a strong management team (from operations to sales and marketing to finance) and focusing on short-term intense projects that took full advantage of Brulant's trademarked "Time to Value" methodology for delivering fast results.

Revenue streams that used to come largely from industry were now diverted to issue from new sources in the consumer/retail, financial services, healthcare and government sectors. Focusing on these industries allowed them to work with higher-level executives, and they began to grow again slowly. Gradually as revenues solidified, they added programmers, products and practices (including business intelligence and Oracle).

Results: 97% growth over last year. Len's thoughts: The company is the people. Help build your own leaders. Hit singles and doubles; don't worry about home runs. Think more critically before you make a decision. Doing the small things well gives a company substance.

We've all heard the advice to narrow your niche and grow.

Celebrating Success!

Len's take on that: Focus on just one or two things – that gets everyone focused. Then don't waste time, just take action.

CARDINAL COMMERCE
Innovation and Reaching Out

What have you bought online lately? A lot of people still can't get past their fear of security issues in virtual purchasing – and that includes a lot of the merchants who want to sell you things! That's because up until now, those merchants have had to assume 100% of the responsibility for any credit card losses that occurred because of fraud in online transactions (where the card itself wasn't used).

Michael Keresman III and his co-founders put Cardinal Commerce on the map with the answer to merchants' prayers. They saw the need, did the research and developed a solution that literally takes the risk out e-commerce for merchants.

The product, which is both software and a methodology, permits credit-card-issuing banks and the consumers who use their cards to write an airtight verifiable contract for every transaction made without a card. The authentication process works with today's approaches and is ready for tomorrow's as well – eye scans, thumbprints, voice recognition, and so on – and can be leveraged for multiple applications such as pay-at-the-pump, biometrics systems, mobile phones, and so on.

When Michael accepted the challenge of making Cardinal Commerce the world leader in authentication services, he applied some lessons he'd learned earlier: pull together a Board of highly experienced business leaders who'll brainstorm ideas, help you map your course, and call you on your mistakes – before they kill the dream.

Conference Stories

His advice to other entrepreneurs: Build a strong foundation. Don't try to do it alone-get the best advisors. Then listen to them. And make sure to leverage your product to create additional revenue streams from different applications, different markets.

CONTINENTAL CUISINE
Mediterranean Restaurant

Everyone in the Sebbagh family cooks – the parents and the sons all enjoy the same skills and interest in healthy food. Noticing at their church's yearly cookout how much the church members enjoyed the Mediterranean foods and being in need of a way to support their parents, the sons decided that owning a restaurant would be a good business strategy.

So, in 1998 they opened a deli style restaurant that allowed for a small number of dine-in customers and provided carry out service. As the business grew, Ata Sebbagh and his family, in the words of the Mayor who presented them with the 2000 Mayor's Award for the Outstanding Eatery, "built relationships with customers that almost equal the quality of the food."

In 2002, they leased the space next to them and expanded into a full service restaurant in addition to the carry out service, allowing them to create a customer environment for more formal dining and increasing the number of people served by between 200 and 300% . Roughly, 40% of their business is delivery/take-out and is facilitated by the new/improved point-of-sales equipment system. The sons both graduated from the University of Akron and are experienced IT people, saving $10K-$17K by modifying the software themselves.

Celebrating Success!

They have learned that it was more work than expected – not an 8 a.m. to 5 p.m. job – and that the growth came from word of mouth - not advertising. When asked what he would tell other businesspersons, Ata Sebbagh feels that being disciplined is as important as having knowledge of the business and also being able to look ahead as well as taking a chance. You must have a good product, spend money the right way, and as an employer you have the responsibility for each employee's well being.

DECISIONPOINT MARKETING AND RESEARCH
Market Research and Consulting Services

During the past few years, DecisionPoint had to react to the economic conditions and reconstruct themselves into a full service research organization. In the past using telephone data and focus groups, the previous company, Data for Decisions in Marketing, Inc. struggled with profitability and growth. In addition, their customers needed strategic insight and were asking for full service – not just data collection services. They decided to refocus and move the business from data gathering to full service: identifying the problem, doing the research and interpreting the data.

During the transition, DecisionPoint created the best video lab in the country and a web usability room that allows organizations to watch and learn how their websites are used. Other products include doing site surveys, along with data mining to evaluate how products are used or to determine other uses for existing products. Lawyers are joining the focus group process for mock jury selections to understand better how juries deliberate. The quality and depth of customer relationships has improved, because clients are changing their business processes in response to the results of their research. DecisionPoint has signed a ten year lease and now considers all of their business relationships as long term – not short term. Cash flow has improved, sales are up 37% from last year and they are now moving into the national market using what they have learned in Northeast Ohio.

Asked what they have learned, Amy Merrill answered, "Treat time as a precious commodity, because it is easy to get involved and let the business suffer. Manage the banks." They found that local community banks were not as supportive of small business as the large regional banks. And what advice would she give? Experienced and secure businesswomen are great mentors. Hire people who are passionate about what they do. Relationships and energy count for everything. Referrals are golden. When things get busy, don't work in the business, work on the business. And always remember, "Your customers are the golden nugget, they typically don't care about what upper management thinks is important – listen to their voice regularly"

INTERACTIVE MEDIA GROUP
Innovation

Leaping to conclusions that pay off is a practice Andrew Holland and his team at EYEMG put to work with consummate skill in their web-development business. In the nine years they've been at it, they've redefined "reinvention" – it's now their middle name.

Originally serving customers as a computer hardware service and computer-based training company, the guys at EYEMG gradually noticed more and more businesses catching on to the Internet as a serious marketing tool. Never the follower types, they

Celebrating Success!

jumped on the bandwagon ahead of many others and, using creative marketing techniques like a sandwich-boarded sales rep walking the Galleria, soon became a premier provider of web design and development to some of the largest industrial companies in the Ohio valley.

Always value providers – and not the lowest-priced ones – Andrew and his team in the last couple of years started noticing something else. As the Internet love-fest filtered down to the mid-sized business, they saw a whole new market in the middle – but realized that cost would be more of an issue for this level of companies.

In true EYEMG fashion, they engineered another transformation: using low-cost, high-reliability open source tools, they developed a do-it-yourself product called "eyemg.Compose" that lets authorized employees add, delete and edit website content and then publish it themselves, saving dramatic amounts of time over previous methods and affording contributors pride of ownership – which always inspires people to do their best and give more, which in turn means companies tend to keep more of their knowledge capital if an employee leaves.

Imagining – and then creating – win-win situations is what EYEMG is all about. Andrew's observations for others: Watch carefully. Look for trends, listen to your customers and respond quickly. Most of all, care.

UNITED SECURITY MANAGEMENT SERVICES, INC.
Security Guards and Related Support Software

Serving companies' businesses in Northeast Ohio since

Conference Stories

1971, the locally owned security guard company United Security Management Services, Inc. realized a need in the marketplace for technology solutions founded on the cornerstone of information and speed. Security incidents and missed guard hours can be costly. "Immediate knowledge is power."

Knowing the importance of instant notification of incidents and deciding to diversify into software solutions that can be sold to other security companies, United Security developed two new products. The Telephone Incident Reporting System (TIRS) provides the solution to transform any phone into a simple to use interface that automates all reporting immediately and implements follow-up response calls to management via phone, fax, pager and e-mail in minutes. The Guard Patrol Information Systems (GPIS) monitors guard tours through automated monitoring devices such as wands and buttons. In the event an exception occurs, such as a missed tour, the system instantly notifies the correct persons via cell phone, pager, PDA and/or e-mail. Clients are now more efficient getting needed information to the correct parties and are able to manage liability and risk. The incident "questions" can be customized for each client. There are a standard eight possible events with eight questions for each event. Used proactively, TIRS also serves as a remedy for preventing repeat incidents.

These new products have resulted in new recurring revenue streams and expanded geographic reach for United Security, along with providing technologically advanced solutions for the entire security industry.

United Security has been surprised with how well TIRS has been received. When asked for advice, Ralph Brislin, EVP, answered, "Don't be under funded. Stay focused!" In hindsight,

Celebrating Success!

they would not have launched the two programs at the same time. "GPIS was sold by an enthusiastic person making it difficult to deliver up to expectations."

UNICALL INTERNATIONAL INC.
Integrated Marketing

In April of 1999, Ben Harris established Unicall International, Inc., the direct marketing and call center company, to provide the marketplace with an expert tele-services resource. Typical of most startup companies, Unicall needed financing, methodology, people infrastructure, business development, marketing support and a sales process. Without a "seed" client the challenge to succeed was daunting.

Unicall has made phenomenal use of technology to attract new customers and grow its customer base, including customers outside the local region. Unicall optimized its website to rank high with the major search engines, ran and runs targeted pay-per-click marketing campaigns, and used e-mail blasts to encourage prospect inquiries. They have been able to provide world-class service and compete with larger call centers, because Harris had the foresight to invest in advanced digital call switching technology. Unicall also has established the design subsidiary, Lunar Cow, with complete turnkey marketing solutions for clients, assuring brand consistency and high quality. They have also built proprietary development tools and a ten-step methodology – time-to-deploy is shortened without sacrificing quality. This provides faster return on investment for both the client and Unicall. Now positioned to gear up the Internet sales channel almost at will, Unicall is experiencing consistent revenue and margin increases. They have

Conference Stories

gained several Fortune clients, word-of-mouth referrals are high and client retention is over 85% . And now, customers have the ability to measure the success of campaigns. Unicall clients realize an industry-defying 10% sales yield on 20% campaign response.

When asked about lessons learned, Harris advises, "Clients value having a complete marketing program and the ability to gauge results. Proactive communication with clients ensures that expectations are exceeded. Getting paid up front minimizes collection effort and cash flow difficulties. Startup managers need a working knowledge of financial metrics and reporting, and especially cash flow management. Develop `business protection' documents early."

TIMEWARE, INC.
Innovation

It morphed three times before Michael Farhat's software reached the shape that's really putting his company TimeWare on the map. From project management tool to insurance quoting mechanism, the market kept pushing him in different directions. At last his product matured into RMS, a biometric (because it uses thumbprints for IDs) product that helps HR manage labor-intensive workforces.

Michael's main concerns were making the product painless to buy and big on ROI. Because he stayed nimble, when he discovered biometric capability he added it immediately and then worked on shortening implementation time from months to days. And talk about ROI: one health care facility saved 10% on it payroll cost and paid for the software in the first month.

Celebrating Success!

While they were at it, Michael and his team came up with another idea: they're replacing traditional time-punching clocks with a biometric equivalent called BioScreen™ that's priced big and selling like hotcakes. The system combines time clock functions with computer smarts and uses touchscreen and audio technology along with biometric fingerprinting to track employee attendance. Even better, it neatly integrates all the functions of its host computer system, including access to all existing databases. That means, among other things, employees can easily view their personal data (accrued vacation, sick time, etc.) at the same time they clock in.

Michael regrets he didn't realize sooner that labor-intensive industries so needed what he could offer – that he didn't look right away for the most painful problems that needed solving. His advice to others: Work hard and be honest with yourself and with others. Be resilient – it's essential to success. Be willing to change based on what you discover.

RADcom, Inc.
Profitability

It's easy to dream, but hard to make it happen. When Bob and Angie Dianetti dreamed up RADcom as a technical writing contracting service, they planned for success and found some, but six years later saw that it wasn't quite what they'd hoped. Never the kind of people to give up, they decided to find out why.

After studying their pricing and profits compared to other companies in the same industry, they realized the advice they'd gotten to change their business model was solid, so they set out to follow it.

Conference Stories

Instead of trying to snag every price-dependent deal that came along, they started focusing their sales efforts on existing customers who already saw value in the products and services they were offering. They raised their prices to accommodate a new guideline for marking 50% profit on every deal.

The advice? Get to the sales fundamentals. Identify what is "good business," then pursue it relentlessly. For RADcom that meant focusing on the fundamentals of the sales process 8 hours a day and doing it with measurable repeatable processes.

They made the leap of faith and found that the new approach and raising their prices really was – even in a cash poor market – the answer to profitability. Their latest revenue report shows a 42% growth in sales, 30% growth in profit, and the highest billings in the company's history.

Bob is happy to share the insight they've gained: You must really believe in your product and service and in your ability to deliver it to those who need it. Then work smarter and harder. And on a personal note: Don't get emotionally involved in your business: remember it's only a means to an end.

SOFTWARE ANSWERS
Innovation

It pays to keep your eyes open. Paul Chaffee found that out when he noticed that the State of Ohio's plan to replace the software in its public schools failed to make progress and lost its funding that's when he and his Software Answers team saw their chance. Tapping into their creativity and significant experience in the educational market, they got work and invented a web-enabled

Celebrating Success!

software called "ProgressBook." Developed with teacher feedback, its captures the newest state-standards educational practices and is quickly becoming known across Ohio as an excellent tool for teachers.

Designed to serve as a grade book, lesson plan and student information system, and the new K-12 software had to be designed to overcome objections from multiple constituencies in the academic community. After piloting it with the Nordonia and Akron school districts, Software Answers submitted a strategic plan and won first place in the growth division of the Northeast Ohio 2002 Business Challenge.

Working closely with the Ohio Data Acquisition Sites (school-owned providers of computer software, training and support for over 95% of the Ohio public schools), Software Answers eventually won over more than 60% of the sites, and they are now also partnering with the Management Council of the Ohio Education Computer Network (the collective of all 23 DA-Sites) to develop a Special Education addition to ProgressBook.

Even though there was a time they were afraid it was all over – they expected to run out of money with 3 months of work left in the project – they didn't even consider failing on the promises they'd made to Data Acquisition. They knew there was nothing else out there that could provide this level of functionality, so they kept the dream alive. Paul says teamwork – the employee bond – is why they made it.

TELL COMPANIES, LTD.
Innovation

Every city has its share of eyesores: structures that once

Conference Stories

housed giant operations and when abandoned become host to drug traffickers and homeless. The decade-long-empty B.F. Goodrich building took that prize in downtown Akron. Until, that is, Paul Tell Jr. and Paul Tell Sr. decided to take a chance.

A new client of theirs, Advanced Elastomer Systems (AES) was moving to Akron in 1994 and needed a secure home for its high-tech operations. Armed only with a vision and determination, Tell Companies bought the B.F. Goodrich building from the city for $1 and set to work.

First, they secured the partnership of several area banks (First Star, First National, Charter One) on what was deemed a risky investment. Then they gutted all but the framework and supporting pillars and grids, and recreated the building with everything from modern HVAC to security systems and, on the inside, even gave AES glass walls.

TellCompanies signed up their own Kids Play as the second tenant because AES wanted its employees to have on-site childcare. From there, the building took off to its current 90% occupancy. When additional parking was needed, Tell Companies built a sky-bridge to adjoining land.

As part of the visionary project, Tell Companies worked closely with the City of Akron, which invested $4 million in recycling/cleanup initiatives to help with the project and in tax incentive programs to bring more new business to downtown.

The finished building, now known as a "bookend" of a revitalized downtown Akron, was a huge personal and business risk for all concerned. Mistakes? Of course. Issues? Absolutely. Worth it? Unquestionably. Hard?

"If it was easy," says Paul Tell, Sr., "anyone could have

Celebrating Success!

done it."

NEIGHBORHOOD MANUFACTURING
Innovation

Neighborhood Manufacturing as both concept and reality came from loss. Neighborhood was Superior Tool Company's nameless manufacturing facility, located in a low income, residential neighborhood on the near west side of Cleveland.

When imports from Taiwan and China resulted in a severe loss of volume, Superior was forced to rethink Neighborhood's mission. The semi-skilled workforce at Neighborhood was earnestly looking for ways to grow and prosper. They cared. "Invest in us and our community," they said. "Train us... we will make you money. We have skills... use them. We have expertise... use us."

Inspired, the owners decided to market and reposition Neighborhood as a separate strategic business unit for Superior. What makes Neighborhood unique is that it takes advantage of the large supply of inner-city workers interested in flexible scheduled work close to their homes. Most of the employees walk to work. Superior implemented an ongoing program to train and develop the employees with the objective of creating a community environment in the workplace. At Neighborhood, the managers of the facility are employees from the neighborhood... an opportunity for leadership that is typically not readily afforded this group at other jobs.

Neighborhood's innovation is more than just a building full of machinery and people. The Neighborhood model was extended with the introduction of Lean Manufacturing and a complete revision of the Employee Incentive System. Lean has led to a cleaner, trimmer company. While the commitment to velocity existed before Lean's implementation, the program has placed powerful tools in the hands of the workforce to operate "on the edge."

So, pick a compelling business topic: The role of manufacturing in the region; outsourcing; inability of firms to hire and retain; the ability of primary manufacturers to differentiate with added value services; or, unemployment. Neighborhood's model suggests alternatives.

PROFESSIONAL TRAVEL INC. (PTI)
Comprehensive Travel Management

As most of us are aware, a combination of events, including Internet sales of airline tickets, the airlines' discontinuation of travel agency commissions, and, finally, the September 11th terror attack all had put increasing pressure on the travel industry.

In order to stay in business and keep their staff, the owners of Professional Travel Inc. (PTI) reviewed their options and decided not to panic and lay off staff. Instead, Mr. Sturm (President & CEO) and his team instituted temporary pay cuts by reducing the hours worked by all employees, making sure that employee benefits would be protected and alternate work arrangements encouraged. Having developed a culture of mutual respect and trust over the years, management knew the value of keeping the lines of communication open with their most important assets - their employees. They were honest about the "new" environment in which they were all working.

Because of financial strength, planning and employee loyalty in difficult times, PTI was able to acquire agencies and some

Celebrating Success!

clients of agencies that were going out of business in the harsh travel environment. They consolidated some of the offices as new employees moved into existing offices, along with opening new offices in other locations in greater Cleveland and the state to accommodate the new business.

PTI knows that both the company and employees can benefit when the culture is built on trust and caring. Employees learned how far the company and its management team would go to keep good workers. A testimony to the success of the PTI focus on their people is that the average tenure of the employees is nine years – a long time for people to stay in the industry. "Working at Professional Travel is more like being a member of a family."

NCS DATACOM
Managed Integrated Network Services Provider

Many service providers offer network management as an "add on" to their focus on providing services such as e-mail, web hosting, and website development. In business since 1987, NCS DataCom looks into the market place and listens to their customers - commercial customers of all sizes - to identify potential needs. They review available technology and either develop or innovatively integrate available services, offering them as individual or bundle service options to their customers.

For example, one recent innovative product release that exemplifies NCS's business approach is the identification and implementation of a secure remote access product (SRA), then adding features to the existing proven technology to provide a unique solution. Unlike most remote access products, this SRA – from Neotris with value added input from NCS – is web based, can

Conference Stories

be made available to businesses of all sizes at a reasonable cost, does not require firewall construction and is compliant with HIPAA security law. The information security is increased because of the capability of identifying work groups and discretely defining accessibility for each.

The NCS team has learned that the customer comes first. When you stay close to your customer, it is easier to identify a need in the market and focus your efforts on solving meaningful issues for that customer. Their primary vision has been to provide the best solution for their customer. They stay focused on knowing their market and controlling their growth so that they don't dilute the value they add for their customers.

Andy Lingenfelter from NCS advises other businesspersons to, "Be flexible when evaluating the market and keep the big picture in sight. A couple of different applications, when integrated, result in a service to be provided. Take traditional proven and stable technologies and use them in creative and unique ways."

ONLYONE
Managed Communication Services

It is a vision of the future of communications that drives Warren Carter, President and co-founder of the cutting-edge joint-venture franchise OnlyOne. The service brings all of your communications into a single number for work, home, fax, cell, pager, voicemail, conference calling, voice messaging and e-mail. OnlyOne allows phone number portability with privacy and complete communications services at cost-effective prices.

In the early 1980s, Carter founded Cleveland-based Voice-

Celebrating Success!

Tel and distributed service through 275 local points of presence – franchisees. Through these vested partners – their local sales of local numbers, one-on-one training and local service and support – the network grew and Voice-Tel was sold in 1997. Most of the OnlyOne Management Team partnered with Carter in Voice-Tel and are anxious to surpass their previous successes. They have an appreciation for the local Managing Partners and have structured an unprecedented joint-venture model of franchising where the risks and rewards are fairly shared. The Managing Partner earns additional equity and managements' compensation is based on the success of the local Partner. OnlyOne is different because of the method of deployment, not the product or technology. To date, OnlyOne has partnered in Cleveland, Akron, Columbus, and Cincinnati, Ohio; Atlanta, Georgia; Denver, Colorado; Birmingham, Alabama; and Charlotte, North Carolina.

When asked what he has learned, Carter answers, "The distribution system is the `magic.' Business relationships have become personal relationships making for stronger real partnerships." He was surprised that it was hard to raise money and has found that most partners were landed through referrals, not through web marketing. Carter advises other business persons "Don't ever quit. Build on a solid foundation. Take whatever time is needed to do it right. Plan conservatively. Multiple financial supporters are an advantage over a single capital source. `Partner' decisions are healthier."

5iTech
Innovation and New Markets

What good is technology if no one knows about it? And there

is no one who can effectively bring it to market? When the former Soviet Union disbanded, scientists there kept on working – and often, our former foes develop some really interesting new technologies. Problem was, the best place to market their discoveries was in the U.S., and with culture, language and distance interfering, the likelihood of that happening for any given project was slim to none.

Leon Polott, a Russian immigrant, educated at Oberlin and the University of Texas Law School, was representing large U.S. companies and a group of Russian physicists when he realized the hidden potential of bringing Russian technologies to the U.S. market – and conceived an idea and a company called 5iTech.

In his practice as an attorney in Cleveland, Leon was instrumental in the establishment of Imalux, Inc., an Ohio-based medical imaging company, with technology imported from the Soviet Union. He decided to take what he'd learned about success and apply it in a systematized way to new technologies he'd uncover. His contacts among scientists and in research centers and labs in the former Soviet Union were more than happy to cooperate.

5iTech selects only those technologies that appear to have strong potential in large markets of $500 million-plus. It follows the legal steps to license and transfer the technology to the U.S. where it then finds access to capital and to licensing partners and helps the new U.S. company bring the technology to market.

Recently the company took on a promising biomedical device product that lets doctors test for allergic reactions before they prescribe certain drugs.

Interest in 5iTech's work is high in the government sector,

Celebrating Success!

especially through the U.S. State Department's non-proliferation efforts. Leon is very pleased his company can promote healthy business interactions between the two former enemies in a way that also creates jobs and new business opportunities for U.S. citizens.

Lessons? Be in the right place at the right time – pay attention and get to work.

MrExcel.com
Microsoft Excel Knowledge and Application Development

If the IT market is down, then how did Mr.Excel.com grow 400%? This is the story of how Mr.Excel.com boomed in a bombed industry.

Bill Jelen was known as the "go to" guy for Excel solutions at Telxon where he worked. With his understanding of the hidden power lying just beneath the Excel desktop, Jelen realized how much time, money and frustration Excel users wasted. He decided to launch MrExcel.com where people could ask Excel questions that he would answer, hopefully generating enough consulting jobs to make as much money as he was in his corporate position.

As the site grew – with Jelen working in shorts and a t-shirt and being there when his kids came home from school – he realized he was still trading time for money. To exponentially increase his revenue while decreasing the amount of time spent programming and charging for the hour, Jelen initiated a plan which included creating and packaging products and services from what he already had (he harvested and indexed over 12,000 questions and answers). He published for a specific segment by creating the ultimate real-world users manual for making sense out of data. He has licensed a simple wizard program for the automotive dealer market that is being used in automobile dealerships.

Jelen stresses that he capitalizes on signature strength by understanding his "crusade" and the emotions his customers go through in using his product/system. He differentiates himself from the competition by knowing who his customers are and building their trust. And he has cloned his system by taking his Excel crusade and building a story and a system around it.

Jelen says, "It's not impossible to see exponential growth. The key lies in sound customer-centered marketing strategy and your expertise and passion for what you do."

GATEWAY TITLE
Reaching Out

You don't always get what you bargained for when you start your own company. Because Rachel Torchia already had some solid relationships with a good number of real estate agents, she figured she could count on their business when she struck out on her own to found Gateway Title Company.

Fate had other plans.

Getting business from existing relationships was to remain a pipedream. What Rachel hadn't counted on was that the agents she knew so well were doing business with her former company for a reason: they liked getting paid for each referral they made – to the tune of numbers that Rachel knew a startup couldn't match – and might never be able to.

Undaunted, Rachel looked into her crystal ball – and did a lot of legwork – to find another approach. Now's the time, she

Celebrating Success!

thought. Time to re-think. Time to get going. When she finally found her answer, she rewrote her business plan to reflect what she'd discovered: a whole new market that wasn't being served.

Turned out most title companies had no interest in working with owners selling their own homes (FSBO – for sale by owner) because they couldn't count on the real estate agents sending them business. In three years, she developed an FSBO title kit, produced marketing collateral, and slowly gained a foothold in the market. She even refinanced to keep the business going.

But she realized she needed something more and couldn't simply wait for things to happen, so she called the Plain Dealer whose readers included her perfect market: owners who want to sell their own houses. It was just the jumpstart her business needed. Rachel is now very proud that she took the bull by the horns and was able to pay back her investors within two years. The lesson: change directions when you hit the wall!

PHYSICIANS MEDICAL SERVICE BUREAU, INC.
Reaching Out

They had a big problem: balancing revenues against growing costs. Physicians Medical Service Bureau (PMSB) had to keep adding more people and more space with every increase in billings. The scales were tipping too far, and after 20 years of steady growth, critical mass had been reached. They knew it was time to do something. Jay Chambers came up with a brilliant solution to his company's problem: let's change the way we do business.

The new approach is based on having customers enter their own data into a web-hosted version of PMSB's software. They had Software Answers create a Virtual Private Network (VPN) so that clients could access systems securely through the web, thus eliminating potential backups with phone lines and keeping clients in strict compliance with HIPAA privacy requirements.

All of that was great news. In fact, because they were able to reduce operating costs so much, the project had a payback time of only 60 days. Even though at first revenues went down slightly, profits went up. But the real kicker was that with the new functionality PMSB had opened up a whole new world of prospects – they could now serve customers nationwide.

PMSB knew that customers always have options. So they made sure all of theirs were allowed to choose whether to participate in the new functionality or keep it the old way. It was critical to put customer desires first, even if it meant letting them walk away.

Jay says tells entrepreneurs to believe in what you're doing. "That makes it fun." And remember, he says, it's okay to charge higher rates and turn down some business. Looking back at what PMSB has just accomplished, he says: "It's good to know that I can decide how much money I want to earn."

FOUNDATION SOFTWARE
Profitability

In the construction industry, as in most, accounting software is one of the first things you buy. Fred J. Ode knew there was nothing more critical than controlling costs and monitoring cash flow in labor-intensive industries, because he'd been helping construction companies with their accounting for years. It seemed natural at some point to write his own financial software – Foundation

Celebrating Success!

Software – and sell it to them.

But the selling wasn't as easy as he'd thought. The first job he got was an hourly-rate gig for a steel contractor for the World Trade Center in 1985. Customers of his former employer's software supported him and his first associates for a long time – 85% of their revenue came from custom programming. But Fred just wasn't sure who else would buy their product or services.

Three years and hundreds of phone calls later, he got his first product sale to a construction customer and got a real start – on the road to the company's current mix of 85% product and 15% services, a much more desirable situation.

In his quest to grow, Fred knew he had to evolve the product – and at some point, bite the bullet and re-write his DOS-based software. He did so in 1990, using SQL Server and adding desirable new functionality. But he knew that no matter how good a product might be, it was always a question of getting it sold.

One of Fred's secrets is to carefully nurture the sales process with a unique approach: he uses an internal sales staff, but because different qualities are valuable in each of the stages of selling – generate/qualify/close – Fred actually uses different people for each stage. He's been so successful – now up to 1500 clients in his totally self-funded business – that 35% of revenue is now new business.

Fred's advice to entrepreneurs: Be the best at one thing. Put people first – have your hiring, education and termination processes firmly in place. And last but not least: Manage by the numbers and watch cash flow.

What else from an accounting guy?...

Conference Stories

OECONNECTION
Automotive OEM Parts Ordering Process and Software

Even though the sale of original equipment (OE) auto parts, along with service and repair, provide a huge business for many auto dealerships, the process of ordering, buying and/or selling OE parts among dealers has been inefficient and time consuming due to the human intervention required. OEConnection with its founding partners, DaimlerChrysler, Ford, General Motors, and ProQuest Company has solved this critical business issue for its customers.

Through a single-source Internet portal and powerful transaction software, OEConnection devised a faster and more efficient way for wholesale buyers to order genuine OE parts and for auto dealers to locate and sell parts. The improvement project took hold on the 7th of December 2000, with the founding of OEConnection. CollisionLink®, a web-based service enabling collision shops to transmit orders for OE parts, was launched in May 2001 to serve the wholesale collision repair buyers. By December 2001, the D2DLink® parts locator and procurement product was piloted and four dealers were activated by February 2002. Initially sold through Ford's corporate program, 4,500 Ford dealers were soon on board accessing an inventory database updated nightly and searching 30,000 times each day. GM adopted D2DLink in mid-2002. In 12 months, over 5,000 GM dealer customers were added to the D2DLink program. Within 22 months of existence, OEConnection became profitable, continues to be profitable for straight nine months and OEConnection is positioned to offer

Celebrating Success!

more supply chain products to the automotive industry.

When asked for a list of lessons learned, Chuck Rotuno, CEO, answered, "Deliver products that solve real problems, not hype. Get the right people on the team. Hire professionals, vs. the fashionable." He was surprised by how difficult it is to change behavior, especially with the collision shop personnel. Rotuno also advises, "You can't try to solve too much too soon. Concepts need to be proven to solve real problems. Control the growth. Never underestimate the value and need for hiring and retaining the best employees. Continuous improvement is essential, especially based on customer feedback. Manage by the numbers!"

FORTNEY & WEYGANDT, INC.
General Contracting (Construction)

Paperwork was a problem. Construction superintendents were inconsistent. It was hand written, not professional and the time-to-office was extremely slow. Dealing with the Project Superintendents who are not typically computer literate, they needed an easy to use system. Bob Fortney, President, and the management team realized that getting better at each and every phase of corporate operations is key to success. If they were more efficient and more productive, the company would be more profitable.

Fortney hired an outside contractor to set up Version 1 of the custom-written SuperView program to process project-specific paperwork. Version 2 was completed by inside programmers. The superintendents are on site daily with the other trades people and sync updated information from the field with a two-week look-ahead schedule maintained. Supervisors now claim they can't live without the system. Information, including photos, is now available daily to all parties needing it. Efficiency has greatly improved and clients can access the information as desired. Superintendents can work offline and update at the end of the day; the synchronization is automated and simple. The surprising part is that Version 1 took hours to synchronize daily, while Version 2 takes just minutes.

Fortney, as the company leader and visionary, has learned that he can't get too close to the details in programming the solution. He advises sticking to the functional specifications and not allowing the programming techies to change anything. Make it user friendly so that it will be used.

Fortney also feels that tangible results = tangible rewards. The way to succeed is continuous improvement; nothing is sacred. Surround yourself with good people and employ a team concept. It is working for F&W. They have won the Silver Hammer Award from *Constuctech Magazine* and the Ernst & Young Entrepreneur of the Year Award.

ICBS, INC.
Web Hosting, Development, and Internet Healthcare

Dr. Jacob Mathew, founder of ICBS, Inc., has found the perfect opportunity to give something back to the community and make a difference in people's lives. Having incorrect data about alternate forms of medical therapy can be life threatening. So, when Mathew's wife, a medical doctor, expressed concern that many patients were referring to Internet for health information and may be receiving incomplete or incorrect information from the web, often biased to promote individual agendas, Mathew decided to develop a website that provides comprehensive information about

Celebrating Success!

all aspects of health (combining traditional western medicine with alternative medicine) including drug interaction concerns when combining herbal remedies, alternative and mind-body therapies and holistic living with modern medicine.

The website, http://www.holisticonline.com (with firstholistic.com and epreferredproviders.com) is now used extensively by general public as well as doctors, nurses, patients and others associated with alternative forms of treatment. The website serves as an in-depth introduction to all forms of medicine including many forms of alternative medicine, and treatment information. It is one of the largest free resource databases of its kind in the world. Mathew is being assisted in this venture by a highly trained team of doctors, nurses, yoga practitioners, herbal specialists, stress management experts, etc. who provide unpaid consulting to ensure the accuracy of the data. Mathew has a library of over 1000 books on the subject so he can use material to validate and plan for new features on the website which has grown to over 50,000 pages of content. It receives over 4 million hits/month from over 170 countries, and has received critical acclamation from all over the world.

Mathew says he has "followed his dream" and wouldn't take money from any sponsors for fear that it might cause concern for the objectivity and independence of the site. With a zero dollar-marketing budget, he promoted the site using search engines and a tremendous effort in networking, personal promotion, and other strategies to push it ahead of sites that have marketing budget reaching into nine digits. His advice to others includes: have passion for what you do, be persistent, believe in what you are doing, be the best at what you are doing and don't copy someone's idea, and don't listen to the people who say it can't be done.

LAZORPOINT, INC.
Network Engineering Services

After being in business for three years, Dave Lazor felt like he was still a one-man operation. He couldn't seem to find the right people. Business growth was stalled - one step forward and two steps back.

Don Steiner was referred to Lazor as a prospective employee and after getting to know one another, they realized they had a shared vision and cultural values. They made one less than successful hire before their streak of good hires. They evaluated what was good in those hires, analyzed, formulated and repeated. They initiated personnel profile testing, identified and codified the company culture and values, and initiated and implemented a branding program. They realized that they needed to build the company, not just billable hours. Clients had always liked the results, but Lazor was approaching burnout by doing so much himself.

Clients are now comfortable with Lazorpoint, Inc., not just Dave Lazor, who is no longer the most important guy to the clients. He is now focused on working ON the business, not IN the business. Clients trust the company – that is made up of great people. Since 2000, the business has grown considerably by every measure: from three to ten employees, tripled the office space with new, higher grade quarters, a full-time office administrator and 100% retention.

Lazor learned that success breeds success. Good personnel hires led to additional good hires. The right people "on the bus"

Celebrating Success!

make all the difference. He shares that he should have done the right things sooner – gained a clear understanding of the company values and defined the culture as soon as possible. Lazor also suggests making investments wisely – don't fear spending according to a plan. Know and measure the numbers. Measure and consider risk and reward. Build confidence in your clients, your people, your business partners and yourself.

MUSTARD SEED MARKET & CAFÉ
Full Service Health Food Store

From a home-based vegetarian catering business started in 1978 with $60 and a cooking pot, husband and wife team, Margaret and Philip Nabors, have grown the Mustard Seed Market & Cafe into the largest retailer of natural and organic products in Northeast Ohio.

In 1981, the Nabors opened a small health food store in Akron's Merriman Valley and named it Mustard Seed Market, drawing from the biblical metaphor that faith is like the tiny mustard seed from which a great tree grows. And the Market grew. In 1989, they relocated the store to an area that was more accessible, had 9K square feet and housed a 60-seat restaurant. Business boomed and in September of 1996, the Nabors made the decision to expand into two stores that became available, adding an additional 22.5K square feet. Upholding the commitment to helping individuals enjoy healthier lives through healthier eating habits, the Market continues to offer an extensive list of cooking classes, lectures and food demonstrations. The success of this store led to another expansion in October 1999 with the opening of the additional Mustard Seed Market & Café in Solon.

Conference Stories

From the beginning, the Market's appeal has been trust - consumers can trust the quality of the food and products they buy. The Nabors spend time on the floor with their customers, know what they want and provide one place where all health food and related products can be purchased.

Their advice includes: putting a process in place that ensures that everyone is treated the same (especially important during growth), visit peers to learn from their success and failures, and hire good people who enjoy their work and then let them do it. It is important to have a higher vision and purpose. Their motto is "together, we'll save the world one bite at a time."

COMPANY CONTACT INFORMATION

5iTech
Leon Polott
1768 E. 25th St.
Cleveland OH 44114

Allergy & Respiratory Center
Dr. John Given
4514 Fulton Drive N W
Canton, OH 44718

Aztek
Kevin Latchford
Director of Sales
26040 Detroit Road Suite 1
Westlake, OH 44145

Bonnie Cohen Ceramic Design
Bonnie Cohen
718 Pine Point Dr.
Akron, OH 44333

Bright.net Internet Providers
Alex Desberg
37 E. Marion Street
Doylestown, OH 44230

Brulant
Len Pagon President
5595 Transportation Blvd.
Suite 230
Cleveland, OH 44125

CardinalCommerce
Christopher Brown
Director of Finance
6119 Heisley Road
Mentor, OH 44060

DecisionPoint
Amy Merrill President
3634 W. Market St. Suite 104
Fairlawn, OH 44333

Continental Cuisine Eatery
Ata Sebbagh
55 Ghent Road
Akron, OH 44333

Fortney & Weygandt, Inc.
Chris Lutjen
31269 Bradley Road N.
Olmsted, OH 44070

Celebrating Success!

Foundation Software
Tracie Kuczkowski
Marketing Director
150 Pearl Road
Brunswick, OH 44212

Gateway Title Agency
Rachel Torchia
8748 Brecksville Rd. #100
Brecksville, OH 44141

ICBS, Inc.
Jacob Mathew President
24 Canton Road
Akron, OH 44312

Interactive Media Group
Andrew Holland President
190 N . Union St. Suite 300
Akron, OH 44304

Lazorpoint, Inc.
David M. Lazor President
14600 Detroit Ave. Suite 1450
Lakewood, OH 44107

MrExcel.com
Bill Jelen President
13386 Judy Ave. N W
Uniontown, OH 44685

Mustard Seed Market
Phillip & Margaret Nabors
Owners
3885 West Market Street
Akron, OH 44333

NCS DataCom, Inc.
Andrew Lingenfelter 2
6391 Curtis Wright Pkwy
Richmond Hts., OH 44143

Neighborhood Manufacturing,
Div.Of Superior Tool Co.
Howard M. Garfinkel
3243 West 33rd St.
Cleveland, OH 44109

OEConnection
Charles Rotuno
President
4150 Highlander Pkwy
Richfield, OH 44286

OnlyOne
Pam Conaway
5755 Granger Rd Suite 630
Cleveland, OH 44131

Company Contact Information

Physicians Medical Service Bureau, Inc.
Jay Chambers
President
6189 Mayfield Road
Mayfield, OH 44124

RADcom
Bob Dianetti
President
1696 Georgetown Road
Unit A
Hudson OH , 44236

Software Answers, Inc. Paul Chaffee President
202 Montrose West Ave.
Suite 290
Akron, OH 44321

TimeWare Inc.
Michael Farhat President
9329 Ravenna Rd. Suite 4
Twinsburg, OH 44087

Unicall International Inc.
Benjamin C. Harris President
3250 West Market Street Suite 205 Fairlawn, OH 44333

United Security Management Services, Inc.
Ralph F. Brislin, Executive V.P.
1440 Snow Road
Cleveland, OH 44134

ABOUT THE AUTHORS

RONALD FINKLESTEIN
President, AKRIS LLC

As a business and technology consultant and coach, speaker, author and Certified Knowledge Manager, Finklestein has both business and technology experience spanning two decades.

Finklestein is skilled in many aspects of business and spends a majority of his time coaching in the 12 Actions Steps to Predictable Business Growth. His forte is helping businesses and business owners understand how to take the next steps in both personal and business growth.

Since 2001, Finklestein has devoted his full time efforts to consulting and coaching as the founder and President of AKRIS LLC, a full service business and technology-consulting firm. AKRIS helps small and middle market companies solve business problems through the focused use of limited resources.

In addition to being a Certified Knowledge Manager, he is also a Certified Document Imaging Architect and was profiled in the 2000 edition of Who's Who in Information Technology.

He founded The Business Leadership Association, NEOSA's Business & Technology Group as well as being the co-founder

Celebrating Success!

& co-chair of the Celebrating Success! Greater Akron Business Conference – Other Board affiliations include: Advisory Board, Center for Information Technology and eBusiness of the University of Akron; Advisory Board, Kent State University Center for Information Management; President of Summit Spiritual Center, Board of Trustees.

Finklestein is available for coaching, consulting and speaking engagement, workshops and seminars. You can contact him at ron@yourbusinesscoach.net or reach him at 330-990-0788. Sign up for his newsletter at www.yourbusinesscoach.net.

CHARLES M. GILMORE
Principal, Avantt Consulting

Before joining Avantt, Chas accumulated over 35 years of high-technology management experience in U.S., European and Asian consumer, industrial, software and aerospace markets.

He worked for multinationals such as Schlumberger, Zenith Electronics and Groupe Bull; for mid-sized public and privately held companies such as Heath Company (Heathkit), Alltrista Corporation and YXLO N International, and for startups.

For the last twenty years, Chas has held senior posts such as COO, CEO and President. His specialty is strategic planning and product development, and he has proven success with strategic realignments. Chas led the successful turnaround and restructuring of a number of firms, as well as overseeing the acquisition and divestiture of product groups and companies.

Known as an out-of-the box thinker, Chas brought change to the organizations he led through unique and highly successful

About the Authors

management structures, business models, and new product-line and product concepts. He also guided the redirection of companies, moving them from decaying late-stage companies in stagnant markets to rapidly growing, profitable second-stage companies in new expanding markets – while still preserving and capitalizing on the brand name recognition, infrastructure and human resources of the original company.

Chas has been involved with a number of not-for-profit organizations both as a member of volunteer executive boards and as a consultant. He served on the board of directors for a regional healthcare organization with three hospitals, two nursing homes, two pharmacies and a durable medical equipment supplier. He also was a board member, executive board member and consultant with a regional economic development organization.

As an agent of change, he redefined roles for many team members, thus allowing them to significantly increase their contributions to the organization. Among his accomplishments, Chas counts over a dozen former employees who are now Presidents/CEOs of their own companies.

Chas holds a BS in Physics from Hobart College and pursued advanced business studies at the Harvard Business School and Wharton. He is also the author of numerous texts on electronics technology (McGraw-Hill), served on the boards of directors for a number of organizations, and is the holder of patents related to electronic instrumentation.

cgilmore@avanttconsulting.com, 330-867-9860

Celebrating Success!

IVANA TAYLOR
ThirdForce Marketing

Ivana Taylor has built a business around making pricing and competitive pressures disappear. She has spent the last 17 years repositioning public, private and equity-funded industrial organizations into new, more profitable markets. She loves the challenge and reward of turning a mature organization in a mature market into a bustling, impassioned competitive force. And so do her clients. Her approach to marketing is grounded in sound strategic principles – but look out for her unorthodox approach to application and implementation.

In 1999, Ivana formed ThirdForce, a strategic marketing firm that provides its business-to-business clients with a unique and profitable market position that makes them the obvious choice for their ideal customers.

Ivana calls herself an instinctive and intuitive strategist. She sees those subtle decision-points that typically make the difference in who your ideal client will choose; you, your competitor or nothing at all.

Ivana's vision is to make her clients the only game in town.

Ivana holds a Masters Degree in Management from Antioch University, a Certificate in German Language Studies from the University of Munich and a B.S. in Marketing from Pennsylvania State University.

Ivana is an active member of the Akron and Cleveland business communities. She is a member of TEC, Women's

About the Authors

Network and National Association for Women Executives. She is also a motivational speaker on team development, leadership and strategic planning.

Ivana Taylor, ThirdForce Marketing 330-472-0981 ivana@ thirdforce.net

THE BOTHWELL GROUP
John M. Bothwell Ph.D. President

John M. Bothwell, Ph.D. is an international business trainer, author, and consultant with over 30 years of national and international sales expertise. Dr. Bothwell has combined psychology with his many years of real world selling and sales consulting experience to help business leaders achieve their goals. Dr. Bothwell is an adjunct professor on the staff of Cleveland State University.

As an aggressive problem solver and recognized industry leader, John Bothwell applies his diverse experience and talents to growing his sales-and management-consulting firm. John leads his team in implementing strategies and tactics that achieve both company and individual growth for their clients. Working with a variety of companies from Fortune 500 to start-ups, he has developed insights and skills proven to be successful in real-world settings.

Celebrating Success!

John M. Bothwell, Ph.D. has ISO certification in sales and marketing and is a certified senior manufacturing engineer with the Society of Manufacturing Engineers. Other International accreditations include Certified in Marketing and Sales (CMS), Certified Professional Behavior Analyst (CPBA), Certified Professional Values Analyst (CPVA) and Certified Attribute Index Analyst (CAIA).

By John M. Bothwell Ph.D.

The Bothwell Group, Inc.

440-356-8774

jmb@bothwellgroup.com

JOSEPHINE GILMORE
Partner/Marketing Consultant, Group Gilmore

Group Gilmore is a private consultancy specializing in strategic marketing for technology products and services. We have over 40 combined years of international experience with technology, from consumer electronics to capital equipment, and we know what it takes to create a sustainable advantage in today's global marketplace. Our services include New Markets & Products, Competitive Intelligence, and Strategic Marketing.

Josephine Gilmore is a multi-lingual marketing strategist with 15 years of international high-tech experience, including e-commerce, telecom, semiconductors and electronics. Her specialties are strategic marketing and market analysis. In addition to her professional work in Europe, Asia and the U.S., she has also taught professional and university courses in ecommerce and marketing.

About the Authors

Ms. Gilmore holds an MBA in Marketing from Suffolk University and a Master's of International Management from Thunderbird, the American Graduate School of International Management. She is fluent in French, and conversant in Spanish and German.

Josephine.Gilmore@GroupGilmore.com, 330-867-1211

CONFERENCE STORIES AUTHOR
CHRIS KING PRESIDENT/OWNER,
Creative Keys

A human development specialist, artist, web site developer and designer, storyteller, trainer, consultant, TV announcer, model, mathematician, marketing manager, newspaper editor, salesperson, waitress, writer, speaker and mother of five are some of the personas that have given Chris King her creative expertise and lots of material for her presentations.

Chris, who has a Bachelor of Arts Degree in Mathematics from Goucher College and all course work toward a Master of Fine Arts Degree in Studio Art from Kent State University, shares that her true passions are storytelling and the Internet.

Chris has appeared in TV commercials; won art awards at the Cleveland, Massillon and Columbus Museums of Art; was named District 10 Toastmaster of the Year -1990-91, by Toastmasters International and received the 1997-98 Chapter Member of the Year Award from the Ohio Speakers Forum (a Chapter of the National Speakers Association).

Celebrating Success!

She is a member and the Ohio State Liaison of the National Storytelling Network, past president, current membership chair and webmaster for the Ohio Order for the Preservation of Storytelling

(O .O .P.S!), immediate past president of the Greater Cleveland PC Users Group, and is a Certified Group Fitness Instructor with the American Councilon Exercise.

If you want more information on Chris' business and/or websites visit:

www.creativekeys.biz (business site)

www.creativekeys.net (information site)

chris@ creativekeys.net

(216) 991-8428

BARBARA PAYNE

A friend once pressed her mercilessly to come up with exactly what she planned to tell the people at a Fortune 500 corporation about what she really does for companies. He kept pressing her, when suddenly she looked heavenward and it came to her. "I help them find their true voice," she said. "...help them express their true meaning in powerful words."

Thus was born the trademarked tagline Barbara now uses on her corporate website and her marketing materials: "Find your True Voice... and grow your business"™

The ability to write, Barbara says, is a gift. What you do with it depends on who you are. She says hers comes with years of experience learning from smart businesspeople how best to answer

About the Authors

WIIFM (what's in it for me?) for her clients' target audiences.

In recognition of her 20 years of accomplishments, Barbara was invited to co-author a book with business gurus Brian Tracy, Mark Victor Hansen and others. The book is called "Create the Business Breakthrough You Want: Secrets and Strategies from The World's Greatest Mentors," and it's endorsed by well-known business giants like Ken Blanchard (One-Minute Manager) and Dr. Stephen Covey (The 7 Habits of Highly Effective People). It's on the presses right now; you can get your copy in September. You can reach her at Barbara@ reallygoodfreelancewriter.com

Barbara Payne, Managing Principal

a ReallyGoodFreelanceWriter.com

www.ReallyGoodFreelancewriter.com

Marketing Tips Blog:

www.reallygoodfreelancewriter.com/GetMoreCustomers/

Business Blog: www.BlogforBusiness.com

Bioscience: www.BioMedNews.org

Cleveland 440.646.0041

Chicago voice mail/fax 312.416.7965

INDEX

Symbols
5iTech 72, 134, 135, 149

A
accountability 61
Advanced Elastomer Systems 129
advisors xiii, 28, 38, 119
Air Tran x
Allergy and Respiratory Center 10, 73, 111, 149
American Express x
attitude 1, 2, 3, 7, 8, 16, 20, 23, 27, 28, 31, 32, 63, 113
Aztek 70, 73, 113, 149

B
behaviors 7, 49, 63, 65, 91
Bonnie Cohen Ceramic Design 73, 114, 149
Bothwell, John M.. See sales
Bright.Net 73, 116, 149
Brulant 70, 73, 117, 149
Budget 55
budget ix, 1, 23, 24, 38, 56, 58, 59, 94, 95, 144
business objectives 21
business plan 3, 4, 12, 24, 26, 69, 75, 138
Business processes 61
business processes 1, 3, 5, 62, 64, 66, 72, 102, 113, 120

business strategy 1, 4, 6, 19, 23, 37–52, 38, 39, 102, 103, 119
buyer behavior. See marketing

C
Campbell, Anita ix
Cardinal Commerce 70, 73, 118
Carter, Warren 133
Chaffee, Paul 127, 151
Chambers, Jay 138, 151
Clarke, John 116
coach ix, 9, 90, 95, 153
coach or mentor 90
communications 50, 113, 133
company culture 1, 7, 59, 99, 102, 145
competitive advantage 14, 16, 43, 74
Conference xi, xii, xv, 61, 111, 154, 159
Continental Cuisine 72, 119, 149
contingency plans 51, 84
corporate culture 3, 7, 9, 11, 57
Corwon, Holly ix
culture 2, 2–4, 6, 7–12, 16, 23, 32, 59, 63, 65, 114, 131, 132, 135, 145, 146
Customer Relationship Management 13

customer service 1, 2, 5, 7,
    13–15, 29, 73, 75, 86, 114

D
DecisionPoint 20, 73, 120, 149
Desberg, Alex 149
Dianetti, Angie 126
Dianetti, Bob 20, 151
Discipline 3
discipline 1, 4, 6, 23–26, 47
Dr. Given 11
dream ix, 11, 28, 38, 83, 106,
    118, 126, 128, 144

E
employee development 12
entrepreneurs 5, 25, 33, 83,
    84, 116, 119, 139, 140
execution. See business
    strategy
EYEMG 121, 122

F
Farhat, Michael 125, 151
feedback 62, 66, 128, 142
financial risk 34
financial roadmap and budget 4
Finklestein, Ronald ii, xv, 153
focus. See attitude
Fortney, Bob 142
Fortney & Weygandt 70, 72,
    142, 149
foundation 38, 119, 134
Foundation Software 73, 139, 150

G
Gateway Title 8, 9, 72, 137, 150
general advice 1, 6, 105
Gilmore, Charles M. 53, 154.
    See also business strategy
Gilmore, Jo ix
Gilmore, Josephine 158
Given, Dr. 10, 111–113
goal. See goal setting
goal setting 29, 56, 83–84
GPIS 123, 124
Greater Akron Chamber x, 99, 100

H
Harris, Ben 124
Hill, Napoleon 27
Holland, Andrew 121, 150

I
IAC ix, x
ICBS xiv, 70, 74, 143, 150
Imalux 135
implementation plan.
    See business process
independence 29, 144
information technology xi, 1,
    5, 69, 69–70, 75, 153, 154
Interactive Media Group 72, 121, 150

J
Jelen, Bill 136, 150

K
Kent State x, 154, 159

Index

Keresman, Michael 118
King, Chris ix, 159

L
Latchford, Kevin 114, 149
Lazor, Dave 145
Lazorpoint 73, 145, 150
lesson learned 25
Lingenfelter, Andy 133

M
marketing 5, 20, 73, 77, 79, 81, 82, 85, 113, 120, 124, 150, 156, 157, 158
Mathew, Dr. Jacob 143, 150
McNamara, Thomas ix
MCPc x
Merrill, Amy 20, 121, 149
methodology. See business process
monitoring 51
MrExcel.com 73, 136, 150
Mustard Seed Market xiv, 72, 146, 150

N
Nabors, Margaret and Philip 146
NCS DataCom 74, 132, 150
Neighborhood Manufacturing 74, 130, 150
Neotris 132

O
objectivity 29, 144
Ode, Fred J. 139
OEConnection 70, 72, 141, 150
OnlyOne 70, 72, 133, 150
organizational knowledge 12
ownership 48, 61, 122

P
Pagon, Len 117, 149
persistence 29
Physicians Medical Service Bureau 73, 138
planning xii, 24, 25, 36, 45, 46, 48, 56, 111, 131, 154, 157
PMSB 138, 139
Polott, Leon 135, 149
ProgressBook 128

R
RADcom 20, 70, 73, 126, 151
referrals. See sales risk
risks 4, 33, 34, 35, 36, 58, 65, 96, 134
roadmap 55
root emotions. See marketing
Rotuno, Chuck 142

S
sales 5, 83, 96, 114, 149, 158
sales risk 33–34
Sebbagh 119, 120, 149
self-confidence 33
selling system 90–92
Smart Business x
social risk 34
Software Answers xiv, 70, 73, 127, 128, 139, 151
standards 70, 128

Steiner, Don 145
Sturm, Mr. 131
Superior Tool 74, 130, 150

T
Taylor, Ivana. see marketing
teamwork 28
technical risk 34
Tell, Paul Sr 129
Tell Companies, Ltd 128
TenthFloor x
their desire. see marketing
Think and Grow Rich 27
TimeWare 70, 74, 125, 151
time constraints 19, 20
TIRS 123
Torchia, Rachel 8, 137, 150
training 6, 99, 101

U
Unicall International 74, 124, 151
United Security Management 74, 122, 151

V
Vacca, Chris ix

W
Westfield Bank x
Westfield Creative x
work/life balance 3

Y
your crusade. see marketing

ORDER FORM

If you would like to order additional copies of this book or want more information to engage AKRIS for a coaching, speaking, workshop or consulting, please fill out the form below and fax to 330-990-0788. Or you can mail your order to:

AKRIS LLC
211 Harcourt Dr
Akron, Ohio 44313

Description	Price	Number of Copies
1-5 Copy	29.95 each	_____
6-10 Copies	26.95 each	_____
11-20 Copies	23.95 each	_____
Over 20 Copies	19.95 each	_____

All necessary taxes and shipping and handling charge will be added to all orders.

Please send all questions to ron@ yourbusinesscoach.net

Ship to Address & Contact Information

_____

_____

_____

_____

_____

Printed in the United States
36647LVS00002BA/82-309